The Last Best
Of All Times

Robert Semenza has always considered himself fortunate to have been brought up in what may have been, in his mind, the "last best of all times"—"an era that spanned only a little more than a decade and a half, from the early forties to the midfifties, from World War II to the Korean 'police action,' from FDR to Harry [the buck stops here] Truman to Ike." He was even more blessed to be raised in an environment where he was "surrounded by a wealth of love and warmth from our parents and a seemingly unlimited number of relatives and "piasians"; however, the adults in our lives were there only when we needed them—sort of a 'Charlie Brown' type of existence but without his anxiety."

He felt that all his wonderful memories would be lost forever and wanted to preserve them for the generations to follow. His tale is told in a self-effacing way and from the perspective of a young boy being raised in "the West," a neighborhood in New Rochelle, New York; "of Italians and colored people" (you never called them "blacks" or "African Americans" unless you were prepared for a fight); and the rest of civilization, referred to simply as the Americans.

It tells of his Tom Sawyer/Huck Finn type of youthful adventures and mishaps centered around a cast of colorful and unforgettable "characters" that roamed the streets of the West, from the likes of the "Goat Man," who would "proudly parade his goats down Union Avenue" and whose "route was undeniably marked by a trail of small round soft black pellets, which the goats expelled as they merrily strolled to their noonday repast [presumably to make more pellets]"—to the "Iron Horse" to Louie "Chicken Breast," and to a whole host of other characters. As he explains, they "were just there and accepted as they were, except that they, like everyone else in the neighborhood, had a nickname, which was generally linked to their physical appearance, which, in each case, was obvious." He has attempted the impossible task of trying to list all of these nicknames—his nickname was "Chesty"—the reader will learn why.

His personal memories transport the reader back to that time and to his boyish recollections of his family, the school, the church, the Boys Club, the games they invented, and the special joys brought by each season of the year.

The Last Best
Of All Times

Robert A. Semenza

Copyright © 2007 by Robert A. Semenza.

Library of Congress Control Number:		2006910066
ISBN:	Hardcover	978-1-4257-4349-9
	Softcover	978-1-4257-4348-2

All rights reserved. No part of this book may be reproduced or transmitted in any form or by any means, electronic or mechanical, including photocopying, recording, or by any information storage and retrieval system, without permission in writing from the copyright owner.

This book was printed in the United States of America.

To order additional copies of this book, contact:
Xlibris Corporation
1-888-795-4274
www.Xlibris.com
Orders@Xlibris.com

CONTENTS

Preface 11

Chapter 1—The Americans 15

Chapter 2—The Longest Day of the Year 21

    The Walk Home from School
    228 Union Avenue
    Martha

Chapter 3—The Endless Summer 38

    (1) Baseball and (2) Baseball
    Other Sports
    Caddying
    Summer Evenings
    Hudson Park
    Oakland Pool and Playland
    Other Trips

Chapter 4—The Games of Summer 50

    Clothespins and Broomsticks
    Inner Tubes
    Telephone Poles and Walls
    Chestnuts and Shoestrings
    Peas
    Cans
    Sidewalks

Wheels
　　　Rubber Balls
　　　Trading Cards
　　　Carnival Games

Chapter 5—The Other Seasons 64

　　Fall:
　　　Back to School
　　　Leaves
　　　Football
　　　The Warrens
　　Winter:
　　　Snowstorms
　　Spring:
　　　Fishing

Chapter 6—The Boys Club 80

　　Movies
　　Activities
　　Halloween

Chapter 7—The Church 89

　　Altar Boys
　　Father Aldo Carniato
　　The Feast
　　Confession
　　The Other Guys

Chapter 8—Clubs and Teams 97

　　Clubs
　　Archbishop Stepinac High School
　　The Crusaders
　　The Mooseheads
　　The Blood Brothers

The Purple Laces
The Foresters
The Sewing Club

Chapter 9—The Aunts and Uncles 114

Uncle Louie
Uncle Tuts
Uncle Jimmy
Uncle Johnny
Uncle Columbus (Bumbo)
Donald Vecchio (Vec)
Uncle Gennero Poggiale (Gennarine)
The Brooklyn Connection
Semenza Family Tree

Chapter 10—The Cousins 126

Ralph DeRosa
Louis Semenza
Richie Semenza
Joe Calo
Armand Poggiale
Johnny DiPippo
Alphonse Poggiale (Fuzzy)
The Car

Chapter 11—Legends of the West 144

The "Whatever You Needed" Man
Home Remedies:
  Worms?
  Overlooked?
  Stomachaches
  Sore Throats
  Amalf
  Backaches and Other Spinal Problems
The Neighborhood Pranks

The Habits
Other Characters:
  Bubba
  Louie "Chicken Breast"
  Stump-and-a-Half
  The Iron Horse
All of Them

FOR MY MOTHER AND FATHER SO THAT THE MEMORIES AND THE LOVE OF LIFE THEY INSPIRED IN ME CAN LIVE ON IN THE HEARTS AND MINDS OF MY CHILDREN, GRANDCHILDREN, AND FAMILY, AND IN THE GENERATIONS TO FOLLOW.

Preface

I had long considered writing about my early formative years in West New Rochelle but never truly found the time to actually do it. Time was afforded to me, however, on my early retirement from public accounting in April 1989, and I decided to take about six months off to try to determine what I wanted to do with the remainder of my life. My first decision was to finally put those early years down in writing, as I believed this would not only be great therapy, but would help me to view my future plans from a clearer perspective. It did. Through focusing on where I came from, I reached the decision to simplify my life by rejecting opportunities to return to the business world and to pursue a second career in teaching at Quinnipiac University. This is a dream I had always harbored, and although it was much more demanding and challenging than I had ever envisioned, it was extremely rewarding and also enabled me to have the time to pursue the seemingly endless avenues of my interests—but that's for another book.

Most of my memories were literally scribbled down in a notebook during the early dawn hours, while sipping one of the several cups of my daily coffee, at our townhouse at Interlaken in Saratoga Springs, New York—what a haven that has been. They were later transcribed onto the first computer I ever had (and still have), an Apple 2E, and later onto the several other computers I acquired over the years. The final editing was done on a Dell Latitude laptop, while sipping one of the several cups of my daily coffee in Starbucks.

I had originally decided to only rely on my personal recollections of those times and not discuss them with anyone, or even go back to visit the West. However, "my book" took a lot longer to write than I had ever imagined, and unfortunately, I had to go back to Cancro's funeral home on Fourth Street several times to pay my last respects to some of those whom you will meet in these pages. I also had to rely on the memory of other historians of the West, my brother Charlie, and cousin Louis especially to ferret out the nicknames of all those great "characters" that roamed the neighborhood.

During the many years I spent in the business world, I would often meet successful men who grew up in the "streets": my dear departed friend Charlie Buondelmonte from Long Island; Joel Ratner from Bridgeport; John Connell from Germantown in Philadelphia; Jack Hennessey from Chicago; Dick "the Leprechaun" McDevitt from Brooklyn; Rick Zimmerman (he actually came from the "country," but I just had to mention him); and others from the Bronx and the inner cities of Boston, San Francisco, and other places. There was always some unique, intangible quality that I recognized in them—a mixture of "street smartness" and a respect for people and the family. I would often draw them into conversations about their upbringing and never ceased to be amazed about the commonality of our early memories. They always spoke of their families and of their parents' tenacious desire to have them succeed in ways they never could. Although they may have been "deprived" of many of the material things we now take for granted, they never spoke of this with any regret. They only reminisced, with boyish enthusiasm, about the multitude of friends they had in the neighborhood and especially of the games they played. Though the games may have been called by different names in various cities, they were all essentially the same ones we played in the West—except I never found anyone who had ever played, or even heard of, "clothespin baseball."

I felt that all these wonderful times and memories would be lost forever, and I wanted to preserve them. Many of the stories that follow will not be new to my grandchildren (Meghan and Maryanne Welch, and Amanda and Robert Scala), as they never seemed to tire of hearing them, especially the names of all the characters that lived in the West.

I found overwhelming encouragement from anyone who would listen to my plans to write my book. I was fortunate to discover some other writings, which I would like to acknowledge.

The first, entitled No One Covered the Fig Tree, was given to me by someone who had given it to them and so on. Unfortunately, the author is anonymous, but I was totally amazed by the many similarities between the memories expressed in those few pages and the story I was planning to relate. I have included it in chapter 1.

I was also pleased to have referred to me a true treasure entitled The History of Italians in New Rochelle, written by Joseph A. DiPietro, MD. Rita Colangelo brought this wonderful book to my attention—she is a niece of my Uncle Columbus "Bumbo" DeRosa, one of the many colorful characters you will soon meet.

The real gems, however, are two books written by a true historian of the West, Anthony (Nooch) D'Ermes, entitled West New Rochelle, NY: An Italian Journey and West New Rochelle, NY: The Italian People. His memories and the depth of research into the families and derivation of so many of the customs that surrounded our everyday lives were fascinating. I even found a few nicknames I had missed; how could I have ever forgotten Ishkabibble?

Finally, to the descendants of the Semenza clan, how lucky you are to be able to put life into those faded black-and-white photos of your ancestors tucked away in the attic? As you will see, each one of them was singularly unique and should never be completely forgotten, but should live on in the hearts and minds of you who follow. This is my gift to you—perhaps you will find something of yourself in the telling.

Chapter 1
The Americans

It may have been the last best of all times to be growing up in America. It was an era that spanned only a little more than a decade and a half, from the early forties to the midfifties, from World War II to the Korean "police action," from FDR to Harry (the buck stops here) Truman to Ike. The era officially ended, however, in my mind on October 4, 1955—you will soon find out why.

But what a time it was! It was the dawn of the nuclear age; the kindergarten for TV; and a time when patriotism was applauded; and words such as crack, AIDS, and terrorists were not a part of the vernacular. It was a witness to the introduction of Silly Putty, Slinkys, Flying Saucers, Ike Jackets, Henry Js, Dior hemlines, nylon stockings. and swimwear named after a tiny atoll in the Pacific, and for which men everywhere will be forever grateful.

It saw the return of the World War II "vets" from the shores of faraway lands, many with "war brides" who would have to be assimilated into a new culture. It "spermed" the "baby boom" generation and inspired twelve million of those vets to go on to higher education under the GI Bill, causing happy college administrators to erect temporary Quonset huts to accommodate the herds, which descended onto their once-peaceful campuses. It ushered in the Marshall Plan to aid Europe in recovering from the devastation of the war and creation of the United Nations. It witnessed the start of the Iron Curtain, the McCarthy era, and the Cold War that would last for over fifty years. It saw the end of food and gasoline rationing, "Dear John" letters from home, Where's Kilroy signs, five-cents beer, and the beginning of one of the largest economic recoveries in U.S. history, as American factories shifted gears from war to peacetime production to satisfy all those pent-up demands.

Although it was a time immersed in a world war, which was preceded by the Great Depression, it was a marvelous period to be raised in and one during which it was difficult for my friends and I to get into any "real" trouble. There were just too many people watching us and ready to run straight to our mothers, the real power in the family.

"Mary, did you know Bobby was down at the dumps yesterday?"

"Mary, did you know Bobby got suspended from the Boys Club . . . again?"

"Mary, did you know Bobby took Yolanda to the movies?"

"Mary, did you know Bobby is going out with a 'Bunny' from PSA?" (I'll interpret that later.)

Who needed the police?

In reality, there was an even greater source of protection—a love and respect for the family, which was so engrained in our innermost being that we could not think of ever hurting or disappointing them. How lucky we, and they, were.

We were also very fortunate in so many other ways. No one had to relocate to another city because of a job change or job loss due to a downsizing, restructuring, or merger. Divorce was rare, and the only single-parent families were generally those where the husband had died, as they always went first.

Although it was not uncommon for both parents to work, this was not the norm; if the woman did work, it was generally in the neighborhood, as it was with my mother. She worked, together with my Aunt Gertie and numerous other relatives, in the dress factory right up the street—it was like having another room in our house, along with another one hundred "mothers" to watch over us.

Growing up in that environment was pure joy. We knew exactly what was expected of us, and the rules were simple and clear. Because of this, there was little doubt as to who we were or where we were heading; we didn't have to ponder this—we just knew. This left us with endless hours to pursue the truly important thing in our young lives: fully enjoying our childhood. We were surrounded by a wealth of love and warmth from our parents, and a seemingly unlimited number of relatives and "piasians"; however, the adults in our lives were there only when we needed them—sort of a Charlie Brown type of existence but without his anxiety.

We never had to think about what we were going to do on a particular day, and we didn't have to ask our parents or consult the TV or cable guide. We had the world at our feet—the West. We had the streets and all the sights, smells, sounds, and, best of all, the characters that inhabited them. It didn't matter that the West measured only a few square miles in New Rochelle, New York, from the cemetery to the south (a revered place not because of the generations of families interred there, but of something that sprung from its hollowed ground: "the chestnut tree." We'll get to that later), to the Boys Club to the north (which, outside of school, was the only structured part of our lives but one which, as you will find, provided me with endless opportunities to undermine its noble attempts to try to build my character), to the Pelham town line to the west (where the "rich people" lived), and to Webster Avenue to the east.

These were roughly the borders of our world of Italians and colored people (you never called them "blacks" or "African Americans" unless you were prepared to fight) and the rest of civilization, referred to simply as the Americans. Again, the way was clear—you were either an Italian or an American. American was simply anyone or anything that was not lucky enough to be Italian, like American bread or American cheese. Americans included Protestants (although I never knew anyone who had ever met one), Jews, and Irishmen (we knew about them because we had a few of each in the neighborhood).

The following anonymous short story expresses these sentiments much better than I ever could:

No One Covered the Fig Tree

I was well into adulthood before I realized that I was an American. Of course I had been born in America and had lived here all of my life, but somehow, it never occurred to me that just being a citizen of the United States meant that I was an American. Americans were people who ate peanut butter and jelly on mushy white bread that came out of plastic bags. Me? I was Italian.

For me, as I am sure for most second-generation Italian American children who grew up in the '40s and '50s, there was a definite distinction to draw between them and us. We were Italians. Everybody else—the Irish, Germans, Poles—they were the "MED-E-GONS." There was no animosity involved in that distinction, no prejudice, no hard feelings—just . . . well . . . we were sure that ours was a better way. For instance, we had a bread man, a fruit and vegetable man, a chicken man; we even had a man who sharpened knives and scissors right outside our homes. They were part of the many peddlers who sold their wares in the Italian neighborhoods. We would wait for their call, their yell, and their individual distinctive sounds. We knew them all, and they knew us. The Americans: they went to the A&P for most of their foods. What a waste.

Truly, I pitied their loss. They never knew the pleasure of waking up every morning to find a hot, crisp loaf of Italian bread waiting behind the screen door. And, instead of being able to climb up the back of the peddler's truck a couple of times a week just to hitch a ride, most of my "American" friends had to be satisfied by walking with their mamas to the store. When it came to food, it always amazed me that my friends and classmates only ate turkey on Thanksgiving Day or Christmas or, rather, that they only ate turkey, stuffing, mashed potatoes, and cranberry sauce. Now, we Italians, we also had turkey, stuffing, mashed potatoes, and cranberry sauce, but only after we had finished the antipasto, soup, lasagna, meatballs, salad, and whatever else Mama thought might be appropriate for that particular holiday. The turkey was usually accompanied by a roast of some kind (this was just in case somebody walked in who didn't like turkey); and it was followed by an assortment of fruits, nuts, pastries, cakes, and, of course, the homemade cookies sprinkled with little colored things. No holiday was complete without some home baking; none of that store bought stuff for us. This was where you learned to eat a seven-course meal between noon and 4:00 p.m., how to handle hot chestnuts, and to put tangerine wedges in red wine.

My friends ate cornmeal mush; we did too, but only after Mama covered it with gravy, sausage, and meatballs. We called it polenta; now it is a gourmet food—Mama must have known it all the time. I truly believe Italians live a romance with food. Sunday was the big day of the week. That was the day you'd wake up to the smell of garlic and onions frying in olive oil, as they dropped into the pan. Sunday we always had gravy and macaroni. Sunday would not be Sunday without going to Mass. Of course, you couldn't eat before Mass because you had to fast before receiving Communion. But the good part was that we knew when we got home we'd find hot meatballs frying, and nothing tasted better than newly fried meatballs and crisp bread dipped into a pot of hot gravy.

There was another difference between them and us. We had gardens—not just flower gardens but huge gardens—where we grew tomatoes, tomatoes, and more tomatoes. We ate them, cooked them, and jarred them. Of course, we also grew peppers, basil, lettuce, and squash. Everybody had a grapevine and a fig tree, and in the fall, everybody made homemade wine. Then, when the kegs were opened, everyone argued over whose wine tasted the best. Those gardens thrived because we also had something that our American friends didn't seem to have. We had grandparents.

Of course, it's not that they didn't have grandparents; it's just that they didn't live in the same house or on the same block. Their presence wasn't that noticeable. We ate with our grandparents, and God forbid, we didn't visit them at least six times a week. I can still remember my grandfather telling us about how he came to America as a young man, on the "boat." How the family lived in a tenement and took in boarders in order to make ends meet. How he decided that he didn't want his children, five sons and two daughters, to grow up in that environment. All of this, of course, in his version of Italian/English, which I learned to understand quite well.

So when they saved enough money, and I never still can figure out how, they bought a house. That house served as the family headquarters for the next forty years. I remember how they hated to leave the house for any reason. They would rather sit on the back porch and watch their garden grow. When they did leave for some special occasion, they had to return as quickly as possible. After all, nobody is watching the house.

I also remember the holidays when all the relatives would gather at my grandparents' house, and there would be tables of food and homemade wine. The women in the kitchen, the men in the living room, and the kids . . . kids everywhere. I must have a thousand cousins, first cousins, and second and some friends who just became cousins; but it didn't matter. Then my grandfather, sitting in the middle of it all, with his pipe in his mouth and his fine-trimmed mustache, would smile; his dark eyes would twinkle as he surveyed his domain, proud of his family and how well his children had done. One was a cop, one was a fireman, the others had their trades, and, of course, there was always a rogue about whom nothing was said. And the girls? They had all married well and had fine husbands, although my grandfather secretly seemed to suspect the one son-in-law who wasn't Italian.

But out of all this, the one thing that we all had for each other was RESPECT. They had achieved their goal in coming to America, to Boston, to New York, to Chicago, or to Philadelphia. Now their children and their children's children were achieving the same goals that were available to them in this great country.

When my grandparents died a few years ago, things began to change. Family gatherings were fewer, and something seemed to be missing. Although when we did get together, usually at my mother's house, I always had a feeling that they were there. It is understandable that things change. Everyone now has families of their own and grandchildren of their own.

Today we visit once or twice a year, or we meet at wakes or weddings. Other things have also changed. That old house my grandparents bought now is covered with aluminum siding. A green lawn covers the soil that grew the tomatoes. There was no one to cover the fig tree, so it died.

The holidays have changed. Yes, we still make the family rounds, but somehow, things have become formal. The great quantity of food we once consumed without any ill effects is no good for us anymore: too much starch, cholesterol, and calories in the pastries. And nobody bothers to bake anymore . . . too busy; it's easier to buy it, and anyway, too much is not good for you.

The differences between "us" and "them" aren't so easily defined anymore, and I guess that's good. My grandparents were Italian Italians, my parents were Italian Americans, and I'm an American—and proud of it—just as my grandparents would want me to be. We are all Americans now. The Irish, Germans, the Poles—U.S. citizens all but somehow, I still feel a little bit Italian. Call it culture, call it roots, I'm not sure what it is. All I do know is that my children, my nieces, and nephews have been cheated out of a wonderful piece of heritage.

They never knew my grandparents.

But back to my story. Each season had its own special feeling and was looked forward to with great excitement and wonderment. Summer was the best of all, and it began with the "longest day of the year"!

Chapter 2
The Longest Day of the Year

Regardless of what the calendar read, the summer began and ended for us on the best and worst days, respectively, of our young lives . . . the end and the beginning of the school year.

The last day of school! What memories that evokes: cleaning the blackboards and clapping erasers for the last time, removing all the captured and long-dead flies from the desk inkwells (ballpoint pens hadn't been invented yet), and wrapping our books in brown paper for the poor sucker who had to use them next year. We never had to say goodbye to our friends because we would see them all summer, but, best of all, we could say goodbye to the nuns; and no one ever saw or wanted to see a nun during the summer. But where did they go? We knew the convent wasn't air-conditioned. Did they just stay in there all summer as a form of repentance for the terror they reined on us during the school year? Did they shed their robes and headpieces and secretly dwell among the Americans? Was there a "Club Med" for nuns? We didn't know and didn't want to know.

The last day of school was, to us, the "longest day of the year." We were always released at noon, and that final bell would send us streaming into the schoolyard screaming with unbridled joy—"free, free"—for almost three whole months. We all rushed home to eat lunch, as no one ever took their lunch to St. Joseph's—there was no lunchroom. Columbus School, the public school across the street on Washington Avenue, had a cafeteria, and we did get to eat lunch there occasionally for reasons that now elude me. It was awful! They served only nutritious "American food," such as creamed spinach; chipped beef on toast; which I later learned was appropriately referred to as shit-on-a-shingle; Jell-O; and, worst of all, evaporated milk.

The Walk Home from School

I would slowly walk down Sixth Street to Union Avenue and savor every step. My first stop would be at Popeye's stationery store to buy baseball cards, mainly for the sticks of gum that came with them—as you will see, I had no need to "buy" the cards.

My next stop would be at Zito's Pharmacy where I would drop a penny into the slot on a scale near the entrance and get a little card with my weight and fortune printed on it. This was a very carefully guarded maneuver, and I always made sure no one was watching, especially one of my friends. I would quickly look at the card and then tear it into a thousand pieces and throw it into the sewer. However, even this printed evidence of my ever-increasing weight couldn't dampen my spirits on this wondrous day of all days.

I would wander into Sacco's grocery store and consider buying a handful of broken cookies from a big barrel he kept in front of the main counter. I would always politely ask him to select them for me, and I wonder if he ever realized that I did this not for any sanitary reasons or because I had good manners, but because his hands were so much bigger than mine.

I would walk past the Tropical Casino bar, which only colored people frequented. It was a marvelous and mysterious place to behold. I would always try to peer through the front door; although I could actually see very little, I could hear sounds of people obviously having one hell of a good time and at any hour of the day or night. This must have subconsciously nurtured my lifelong fondness for bars, bartenders, barflies, and other denizens of drinking establishments—which I would later drift into, and at times stumble out of, in various places around the globe.

Sometimes a fight would break out in the bar and carry over into the street, where knives might even be flashed. We would watch in utter fascination but never saw anyone get seriously hurt. The fight usually included a feisty miniature woman who used only one-syllable words I could never find in the dictionary (like "mudfucker" and "sombitch") and who always seemed to be sporting two black eyes. The most amazing thing about the inhabitants of this bar, however, was their attitude toward the Italians who lived in their midst. Racial tension did not exist, and we lived in harmony and mutual territorial respect. This must seem unbelievable to those living in similar surroundings today, but it was so in that age and in that place. If my mother and aunt happened to be walking by during one of these forays (they worked in the dress factory next store), everyone would stop fighting for a moment to let them pass, politely tip their hats, and greet them good day, only to go back at it again as soon as they had gone a safe distance away—unbelievable but so.

The most wonderful thing about that bar, however, was what could be faintly viewed though a small window, which I was just tall enough to peer through: the first television set I had ever seen. I would stare at the tiny images on that small round screen for hours. Try to imagine what it meant for me to actually "see" for the first time, in living black-and-white, my baseball heroes whose antics I previously could only imagine through the magic of radio and the vocal artistry of:

> Red Barber, describing how Oiskin (Carl Erskine) had the hitter in the "catbird" seat,

> Mel Allen, shouting that Joltin' Joe DiMaggio's shot was "Going, going, gone," and

> Russ Hodges, screaming in the fall of 1951 the phrase that will forever ring in the ears of all Brooklyn Dodger fans, "The Giants win the pennant, the Giants win the pennant, the Giants win the pennant."

I would slowly cross Third Street, which ran between Washington and Union avenues, and dreamily gaze up the street thinking of the myriad of pleasures it would hold for me and my friends all summer long. Charlie "the Jew" Lerner, had a small grocery store at the corner of Union Avenue and this wondrous street. The grocery store was later replaced by a Laundromat where I was to eventually land my first real job, freeing me forever from the torment of caddying (more about that later). It was fun trying to guess the difference between white and colored clothes, although I never understood why this distinction was such a big deal to the ladies (you never saw a "man" in there) that came in with their large bundles as long as they all were cleaned. Other stores that I remember on the corners of Third Street and Union Avenue were the Three-star grocery store and Zito's butcher shop.

Next to Charlie's was a small commercial space that housed a number of minor businesses over the years, including a barbershop; however, none of them lasted long enough to be considered part of the neighborhood. This was followed by an alleyway next to an apartment house where my best friend, Billy Williams, lived. Billy, whose actual name was Vito Guglielmo, lived on the second floor with his mother, who had the "power" (we'll get back to that), and his five brothers and two sisters. He was an amazing athlete and, although slight of built, was extremely fast and had very quick reflexes. He was always one of the first to be picked when choosing sides for box ball or any of the other games we would invent.

His father had died at an early age of a heart attack, a fate that unfortunately afflicted most of the men in their family. I can vividly remember going to his grandmother's house on Washington Avenue to help him bring coal from the cellar of her tenement up to her small apartment. Her rooms were filled with pictures of all her sons whom she had outlived, and there were little vigil candles in front of each picture—that was creepy.

The Williams family lived next door to the landlord, known only as Hankie Noto's Father, and how we feared him. There was a bright side to him, however: his daughter Suzie.

On the ground floor of the apartment, and directly across from our house, was the Cake Shoppe! The store was owned by Louie "the Cake Shoppe" (Celestino), who ran it with his wife, Mary; and a day wouldn't go by without our having something delicious from that shop—from sugar and crumb buns (my brother Charlie's favorite) in the morning, coffeecake in the afternoon, to a charlotte russe at night (a marvelous soft sponge cake topped with whipped cream and served in a small white paper wrapping). Is it any wonder I had a weight problem?

Mickey Moonlight's stationery store was next to the cake shop. Most of our carefree days and nights were spent either in, or in front of, this store. I was always in awe of Mickey (Facazio), as he was very "street-smart" and always seemed to enjoy having us around—and we were around a lot, especially when his beautiful daughter, Rosemary, and his son, Joey, were there.

My cousins Joe and Looch Calo, and their son Joseph, and Johnny ("Dipip") and Rose DiPippo, with their two children, Johnnyboy and Carolyn, lived over Mickey Moonlight's store. The boys were like little brothers to me and would love to tail along, especially when I went fishing. Carolyn was a special favorite of my cousin Ronnie, and he was always carrying her around in his arms.

Directly behind them was a chicken market, which was owned by Leo "the Chicken Market" (Luiso) and his wife, Lena. They had three sons and four daughters, the oldest of which, Lilly, was my first love—Suzie Noto was too old for me. Unfortunately, her older brothers saw to it that my infatuation remained unfulfilled.

That chicken market was truly something to behold—from the cocky chickens scrambling for position in long wooden crates, to the assembly line where they got "processed." This was the only store our mother would send us to where we would gladly go. It was fascinating to watch Leo and his family at work. We would never tire of seeing him grab a chicken from the crate; quickly end its cackling with an expert flick of the wrist; hang it by its feet to let the "you know what" drain out; run it over a Gattling-gun type of a machine to defeather it (my favorite part); dip it in boiling water (I don't know why); remove the innards, which were packed separately; and dissect the finished product, which was wrapped and placed in a large brown paper bag. Now that was a lot more fun that buying frozen parts from the A&P!

Next to the chicken market was Mr. Cirillo's shoe repair shop. I can still remember the smell of polish and leather from that store and visualize him expertly putting new heels and soles on our shoes.

Caruso's grocery store was directly across the street at the southeast corner of Union Avenue and Second Street. Mr. Caruso had six sons, and they all worked in the store, of course. It was packed with everything we would ever need, especially during the food rationing days of World War II. One member of our family was in and out of Caruso's at least twenty-five times a day for bread, milk, soda, candy, etc.

Before a fire, which gutted the entire first floor, there were two stores—a shoe store operated by an elderly man, Musta Geed, and the Caruso grocery store. I vaguely remember that fire, especially all the rats that ran out of the building. The building also included a dress factory, a social club, and a firehouse at one time or another, as well as a banquet hall. Wedding receptions and other celebrations were held there when, in all likelihood, North Italy Hall, which was located on Fourth Street, wasn't available. North Italy Hall's most memorable feature, at least for me, was a small window through which they would pass out sandwiches and other goodies during an affair—that was great, and we would try to get a free treat even if we weren't on the invited guest list.

This building, which was located at 222-4 Union Avenue, played an important role in our family history, as it was actually owned at one time by my mother, who also owned the adjacent home, where I was born and raised. I was not aware of this until I discovered certain documents that I had kept relating to my parents' "estate." Her father and mother, Raffaele and Maria Guiseppe (whom I discovered in those documents died on February 10, 1934—when my mother was carrying me. My eyes filled with tears when I made this discovery thinking of how difficult it must have been for her at that time), had purchased both properties in 1925, I believe, and later transferred them to my mother—did my father luck out! Although they were able to keep our home during the Great Depression, they did lose the adjacent property.

228 UNION AVENUE

Above is a photo of our house that stood at 228 Union Avenue. (How that number has never deserted my memory even after not thinking about it for so many years!) We were in the middle of the block between Second and Third Street, next door to Caruso's grocery store, and this small stretch of neighborhood was in many ways its own village—there wasn't much we couldn't get within a stone's throw of our front steps.

We lived in a two-family white stucco house. My family lived on the second floor, and my Uncle Louie and Aunt Gertie (called Trattie by my father) were below us with their two sons, Louis and Ronnie. They were, of course, my first cousins but were actually much more, as in addition to our fathers being brothers, our mothers were sisters! We were, therefore, more like brothers than mere cousins, and everyone would always get us mixed up. They would invariably ask, "Now, Bobby, or are you Ronnie? Is your mother the tall one or the short one?"

We had a four-room apartment (in which I was physically delivered on June 8, 1934), which at one time or another housed my mother's parents (I can still remember my grandfather being waked in the living room) and assorted uncles, as I am told she "took in" my father's single brothers when his mother passed away (how times have changed.) She truly had a heart of gold and was happiest when her kitchen was filled with people and the sounds of their chatting and sipping coffee from a pot that was always on. The bus stopped in front of Caruso's, and friends and relatives would get off and head straight to our house. Visitors to the house were referred to as "company," and that they were. It was a time when people relied on one another for their entertainment, their support, their comfort and, most importantly, their love—company! I can never remember my parents going to a dinner together or to a movie or a play. They had no need for anything outside of their family and friends. How fortunate and undeniably happy they were.

Aunt Gertie's life was filled with certain sorrows having lost our "baby sister," Carmela, as an infant and having Uncle Louie die in his early fifties after a long bout with emphysema. Her days were as full as my mother's, and they were inseparable. For my brother and cousins, it was like having two mothers.

Following is a photo of my parents on their wedding day:

Here is a photo of the bridal party; the only ones Charlie and I were able to identify are (from left to right and from the top row down):

Top row, third, Uncle Tuts; second row, first, Uncle Jimmy; far right, Fannie Cestone and her husband behind her; first row, flower girls, Aunt Lena and Aunt Gertie.

Following are the earliest photos that I have of myself—it should be obvious that my mother had planned to have a girl.

The first memories of my childhood revolve around one theme: being separated from my parents. I distinctly remember three traumatic events involving a car, a zoo and a giant bird.

Actually, the first took place in "the car," which you will hear about later. I have no idea how old I was but apparently not old enough to accompany my parents and brother on a trip to Washington DC. There is absolutely no doubt in my mind that this is the farthest trip my father was to ever take in the car or, for that matter, in his lifetime. It is inconceivable to me that my mother (it had to be her idea) was able to talk him into it. I can still picture myself settling into the middle of the backseat when my Aunt Gertie took me out of the car in order to get an ice cream treat in Caruso's grocery store; of course, I went along with her. When we returned, the car was gone! They did bring me back a "guilt gift": a beautiful white stuffed cat.

The zoo was the famous Bronx Zoo, which I was to visit many times throughout the years. My first recollection is of merrily walking down "the yellow brick road," only to suddenly realize that my parents had taken another path. I can still recall being "grilled" by the park rangers in the "lost and found" area of the zoo. Although I can't remember the relieved faces of my parents when they saw me, I do know exactly what I was doing at that moment—eating an ice cream cone.

The giant bird was an eagle that was in a cage at the Bronx Zoo (that again?). I apparently had gotten my parents so annoyed at me that my father warned me that if I didn't behave, the eagle in the cage near us would take me away. I must have really pissed him off. Defiantly, I walked to the front of the cage and shouted to the eagle, "Go ahead, see if I care. Take me away," to which it responded by spreading open its giant wings, sending me screaming back to my parents. To this day, I do not get too close to eagles.

My father—known, among other names, as "half-a-day Charlie"—had little aspirations but simply lived each day with such enjoyment and happiness, which, in all my life experiences, I would never find in another human—he was truly content. He had held a series of colorful jobs in his younger years, including a conductor on the trolley line, which ran from Mount Vernon to Yonkers, and where, "Little Anna" Libertino told me, he met my mother. Little Anna lived with the DeRosa family (you'll meet them) after her parents died and was also very close with my family. She was at my parents' wedding reception at which the Ferrara family provided the pastries and cake. They were friends of my family and still have their famous pastry store in the Little Italy section of New York City, where my father was born. Little Anna was also to remind me, at one of the many wakes I attended at Cancro's Funeral Home, that while the wedding reception was being held, all the wedding presents were stolen from my parents' home. She intimated that although everyone suspected who the thief was, no accusations were ever made, and she would not tell me who was under suspicion.

My father also had a butcher shop on Fourth Street and at one time worked in a macaroni factory, where he quit because he was the only one who wasn't family, and they all treated him as if each were his boss. Incidentally, the term macaroni, as well as gravy, have been largely lost to the English-speaking races and replaced by pasta and sauces, both of which now come in infinite varieties and are accompanied by outrageous prices. This has unquestionably resulted from the discovery of this unsurpassed, delicious, and once inexpensive dish by the Americans.

Unfortunately, for Charlie and I, somewhere along the line, my father picked up the rudiments of barbering and tailoring. To this day, I prefer going to the dentist rather than the barber. In my mind's eye, I picture myself sitting in a chair in the middle of a steaming kitchen, covered with a sheet and smothered with talcum powder, while my father endlessly pursued those last few "cat hairs," as he called them, with a hand-operated clipper. It would always jam and catch my hair between the dull blades, causing me the most excruciating pain. It only seemed to jam as he was proceeding up the back of my head. As anyone who has ever been led out of a desk seat by a four-foot nun pulling on those tiny hairs can attest, the way to get you to react was to slowly guide those hairs in an upward direction—down doesn't matter as the nuns must have learned in their basic training!

His tailoring skills taught me an early lesson in tolerance and patience, which some claim was wasted on me, as I endured countless sessions of the letting out of my pants and jackets (they never had to be taken in). I hated it when it was time to buy new clothes, as this invariably resulted in a trip to the "husky" section of a store, generally, Barney's in New York City.

My father—who changed his name from Angelo to Charles because he didn't like his given name (but not legally, which, of course, means that my brother actually isn't a junior, as he was always called at home, and his later son-to-be, Charles III, isn't really a III)—finally landed the golden job of the early Depression years: a life insurance salesman for the Prudential Insurance Company of America. As some of his would-be competitors told me in later years, no one in the West would ever consider any insurance salesman other than Charlie Semenza. He didn't even have to try to sell insurance as the neighbors would come to him, and many would even bring the premiums to our home every month. I would watch with utter fascination as he would neatly enter the payments in his huge "debit book." Perhaps this is what eventually led me into the world of numbers (as an accountant and not a bookie). The only part of the job he disliked (he couldn't hate anything or anyone, except for one individual, who shall remain nameless, who my father claimed was the only two people in the world he hated) was Friday mornings when he had to go to the office for a half-hour staff meeting. I once asked him if he ever worried about anything, and he laughed and replied, "Me? I don't get paid to worry; that's my boss's job!"

My mother, whose maiden name was Mary Codella, was a bundle of energy and, although she had only a grade-school education (I believe my father only went as far as the fourth grade), was as sharp as a tack. She was born in Calitri, Italy, in 1898, and her family came to America in the early 1900s. She had one unflappable aim in life, namely, to see her two sons become the first members of the Semenza family to go to college, or she would (and often did, for many other reasons) crack a wooden spoon over our backs. Charlie was the first to go on to the halls of higher education, earning him the nickname "Joe College" from Joe Calo (you will meet him).

Here is a picture of her family with her on the left and followed by her mother, who is holding Aunt Gertie's hand, her father, and her brother, Uncle Vito.

Uncle Vito was married to an Irish woman, Aunt Catherine, which earned him the nickname of "Murph" from my father. They lived in an apartment house in the downtown area of the city; I always loved to go to their home and visit with my cousins, Ralph, Mary, Rosie, Johnny and especially Billy, who suffered from shell shock, which he brought back from his service in World War II. He was always working on model airplanes, and the apartment was permeated with the aroma of glue—no, that wasn't the only reason I liked to visit them.

Uncle Vito was a plumber and, of course, the only one my family would ever use, although I honestly do not remember him actually finishing any job he started. He definitely had a great "love of the grape" and other related beverages, and we just never knew when he would show up to continue working on one of his never-ending projects. I particularly remember that even after the death of my parents, we still had a leak over the shower ceiling, which he worked on for decades.

On the day my daughter Karen was born in New Rochelle Hospital in 1962, my Aunt Catherine died in the same hospital. I was always struck by the irony of this, especially as their given names had the same derivation.

My mother would get up early in the morning to make our breakfast, dash off to work in the dress factory, come home to make us lunch, dash back to work, come home to make dinner, and then spend all night entertaining company. The absolute highlight of her week was Wednesday night—when the "sewing club" met. You will hear more about this auspicious group later.

There is no question that the most important aspect of my family's life was centered on eating, especially on Sundays and holidays. The main feature of many of our meals was, of course, macaroni and gravy—and not the version that came in a jar. My mother would make the gravy by starting with "tomato paste" and then adding meat and various other ingredients, which would simmer on the stove all night. These meals would officially begin around noontime (I would have to "taste" everything much earlier than that) and would extend into the early evening; we wouldn't bother to leave the table as lunch would simply blend in with dinner.

These feasts would generally be held downstairs in Aunt Gertie's kitchen (why?), and she and my mother would never sit down until all the men were served—have those days been lost to civilization forever! I was to be the first one of the four boys to bring a girl into our world: my wife-to-be, Marie Vaccaro. She never tired of telling the story of the first time she was invited to eat with my family, and how we all rushed to the table when dinner was served, including me, leaving her meekly standing next to my mother and aunt. My father put his arm around her and told her that if she wanted to be a part of this family, she had better learn to "dig in" and not wait for an invitation—she was a fast learner and was soon "elbowing" her way to the table.

Birthdays and other parties were generally held in the "cellar." What fond memories I have of the times spent in those damp surroundings, which consisted of a "main hall," a coal bin, a small storage area, and a second room. My father never had any desire to have a "finished basement" as that would have required some maintenance. All he had to do was to sweep the floor once in a while, and we were free to do whatever we wanted as long as we stayed away from the furnace.

On one of the walls was an oil painting of The Storm, which had been done on velvet by an unknown artist (at least to me). It depicted a scantily dressed couple fleeing from an impending storm with only a thin veil over their heads for protection. I have no idea how my family acquired it or why it was hanging in the cellar rather than in a more appropriate part of the house. In later years, I tried to sell it through a "consignment shop"; however, it went out of business, and the painting was never returned to me. I have since seen prints of this picture displayed in various "mall stores" many times and have always wondered if perhaps they closed the shop as they had made enough from its sale to retire.

Although we never ate there, another of my favorite places in the house was the attic. The stairway to the attic was at the end of a long hall, which was outside the door to my family's second-floor apartment. In the hallway were a Singer sewing machine (which was used quite a bit by both my mother and father, mainly to let my pants out) and a portable closet. One day my friends and I were playing in the house after school when we heard a knock on the door. We opened it to find a man standing in the hallway who explained that my parents had hired him to fix the sewing machine. We had no reason to doubt this even though none of us knew who he was, and we went back to whatever game we were playing. Suddenly we heard a scream in the hallway; it was my mother. We opened the door and saw her standing over the sewing machine, which was now largely disassembled. The "sewing machine repairman" was obviously there to steal it and must have been frightened off by something before he was able to complete his caper. Believe it or not, crime was just about unheard of in the neighborhood, at least any that might be afflicted on us, and we naively allowed a complete stranger into our home—that's scary!

My mother and father were both to die in their early seventies, and how I have missed the love and strength they gave me. A day hardly goes by when I do not think about them and wish they could have been here to see my children and grandchildren grow up and to seek their comfort during the difficult times in my life. After almost forty years, I can still see them as clearly as though they were standing beside me, and I believe they are still nearby. My brother Charlie's wife, Terry, once said to him and me that they never truly died because we constantly talk about them, particularly all the "sayings" my father had, many of which I have captured in these pages.

Martha

Adjacent to our house lived one of the more famous inhabitants of the West: Martha! Everyone knew Martha (Jeffers). I never knew where she came from—she was just there. She was a heavyset colored lady who lived in a one-room "shanty," which had been previously occupied by a band of gypsies (I kid you not). I have no recollection of them except for tales from my father and mother, the most famous of which was a legend that Charlie's hair had turned "kinky" after they poured salt on it. This was some type of gypsy revenge they extracted from him for beating up one of their little ones.

At any time of the day or night, someone would drive past her front door and shout, "Marthaaaaaaa!" She would either be sitting out front or peeking through the front window and would shake her fist at them. This may seem cruel, but in reflecting back on it, I believe she truly enjoyed all the attention. What else did she have? She was very kindly to us and, in some distant way, took the place of the grandmothers we never knew. She was always looking out for us, especially for her favorite, my cousin Ronnie, whom she called "Lonnie." We would send "leftovers" to her on the pretence that they were for her cats, and she would say, as my father would love to mimic, "Ma cats? I'm gonna eat this myyyyself."

Next to Martha's shack were a series of low-lying buildings that were generally vacant. However, at one time, the building next to Martha's shack contained a second-hand clothing store operated by Andy Cohen. Charlie and Louis used to hang out in the store, and one Easter, both of them bought fedora hats for one dollar each.

I believe Mr. Charlie Rose owned all this property including a large plot of land adjacent to our backyard, which was dominated by a huge (or so it seemed to me) cherry tree whose limbs would, at times, reach right into my bedroom window. My brother and I shared the room, and we could actually pick cherries straight off that limb, if Charlie Rose wasn't watching; however, he usually was. He was very protective of that garden and got annoyed if a dog or, even worse, we kids should step on his hallowed ground. He looked a little like Popeye, spoke broken English (as did many of the grown-ups in the West), and would always complain about this to my father. My father, who seldom took anything too seriously, once advised him to post a sign proclaiming, "No dogs or kids allowed." Charlie thought this was a great idea until it dawned on him that, in his own words, "But, Charlie, dogs—they no-a-cana-read."

A small house stood at the back of the garden, where Jackie Wells, his mother, and sister Shirley lived. What a warm and friendly family they were. Their situation was similar to a lot of the colored families who lived in the neighborhood. Although many were single-parent households and did not seem to be as "affluent" as compared to the Italians, they had a very strong family life. Incidentally, I always thought we were "rich" as we always had anything we needed or wanted (almost). We were, of course, very rich in the facets of life that truly matter.

An apartment house stood at the southwest corner of Union Avenue and Third Street, and some of the residents I remember are the Telesco and the Cagliastro families. However, the most memorable occupants of this house were Red Hollis, a colored guy; his sister and father, and his dog known only as Red Hollis's dog—we'll get back to that dog. On the ground floor of the apartment was a fish market. What I would now give for the delicacies that lined those frozen shelves: the shrimp, scallops, bacala, clams, flounder, and bluefish. Eating fish in those days was a penance, and few ate it by choice. It was something forced on you by the church on Fridays. I often wonder if all those "sinners" who just happened to get their final calling on a Friday while enjoying a hot dog got to fly out of hell and up to heaven when the church changed that law. My father always claimed the law was only put in because most of the disciples of Jesus were fishermen.

While I'm on the subject, whatever happened to limbo? It has just disappeared from the church teachings. Where have all the unbaptized babies, which the nuns told us were there, gone to? Where have all the pagan poets and other famous non-Christian historical figures—such as Homer, Virgil, Aristotle, Plato, and Cicero, whom Dante, in The Divine Comedy, claimed were there—gone to? I guess I'll just have to wait until "you know when" to find out.

I did, however, remain a holdout and absolutely refused to have any of those denizens of the deep invade my stomach. I even refused to have the scent of anything from the sea violate my nostrils and would parade around the house with a clothespin attached to my nose while the kitchen was saturated with the aroma of fresh giant shrimp boiling on the stove. I survived by eating pepper-and-egg sandwiches and macaroni and ricotta cheese. My mother must have looked down and smiled as I, in my grown-up years, was to scour the world in search of anything to eat that either swam, crawled, or propelled itself through the ocean, from "standing pomfret" in India, to "pacu pacu" in Hawaii, and to "skate wings" in Boston.

My family also followed a tradition on Christmas Eve of eating a variety of twelve different types of fishes. Why? We were also forced to swallow a spoonful of lentils on New Year's Eve, which was supposed to bring us wealth in the coming year. Who needed money when we had our family?

When I arrived home from school for lunch, usually consisting of a bologna sandwich and a Pepsi cola (the real thing, as diet drinks did not exist at that time), my mother was always . . . always there. She would have my lunch ready, and it was always a special treat because I was able to listen to her soap operas on the radio. (Italians only had them in the kitchen as this was clearly the most important room in the house.) Who could ever forget?

- Our Girl Sunday—the story that asked the question, "How could a girl from a little mining town out west find happiness as the wife of a wealthy and titled Englishman?" We never did find out.
- The Adventures of Helen Trent—how we rooted for Helen to end her suffering and marry that shithead Gil—she never did.

I always missed the last part of these never-ending ministries as I rushed to make the afternoon bell but not on the last day of school. I would leisurely change into my overalls (jeans), T-shirt, and Keds (sneakers), and wander out to the front steps. We had a very large porch, but this was usually the domain of the adults or for our use in their company. I would meet my friends to consider the endless variety of pleasures that awaited us all summer long. Even if we didn't actually get to do something special on that particular day, we were allowed to stay up late under the warm glow of the streetlamps and in the shadows of our warm, marvelous old houses and apartments. I wouldn't even bother to go in to listen to any of my favorite radio shows: Tennessee Jed, Jack Armstrong, the Green Hornet, the Shadow, the Lone Ranger, or Martin Block's Make-believe Ballroom. I would even miss Marty Glickman's nightly recreation of the day's Dodger game, which he would "replay" with simulated crowd noise and the crack of the bat against the ball. When our mothers finally called us in (fathers never called us in?), we were content to go right to bed and drift off to sleep. We knew it was the end of the longest day and the beginning of "the endless summer."

Chapter 3
The Endless Summer

Summer meant two things, the two most all-consuming things in my young life:

(1) Baseball and (2) Baseball.

To fully appreciate the significance of this, you must, first of all, understand that this was unquestionably the golden age of baseball in New York. We had the hated-and-despised Yankees in Yankee Stadium; and, across the Harlem River, the hated-but-tolerated Giants in the Polo Grounds; and, bow your head in reverence, the Brooklyn Dodgers in Ebbets Field. You must be tolerant of me in this regard and appreciate that (at least in my maturing mind) no one in the entire history of the world could approach the agony and ecstasy that I endured as the only—yes, the only—Dodger fan that I ever knew in the West (except for my brother who only liked them). Now for those of you who were brought up in any of the five boroughs; Westchester, New Jersey; or anywhere near the Metropolitan area during those years, try to imagine what it was like for me to have to argue, not discuss, the merits of Snider versus Mantle versus Mays from dawn to dusk every day of the year, and to be the only one, against seemingly thousands, to defend the honor of my Bums. Try to further imagine what it was like to have to walk the streets after each Yankee-Dodger World Series with only one retort, "Wait till next year."

But did next year finally come—1955! Magic filled the air that fall featured by the pixie face of Johnny Podres, the amazing catch of Sandy Amoros, and the daring base running of Jackie Robinson. I sat alone in front of the TV (which we had by then) on that unforgettable date: October 4, 1955. I would take no calls or allow any visitors as I sat in tense anticipation, believing that somehow, just somehow, Pee Wee (Reese) would muff that last ground ball or Gil (Hodges) would drop a perfect throw. But they didn't. I was stunned. Wild fantasies of revenge welled up in my brain, and I ran screaming into the quiet, deserted streets searching out all those tormentors of so many years gone by, years that now no longer counted, and phoning those I couldn't find. In a few hours, I purged my soul of all the bitter memories of Don Larsen's perfect game, of Sal "the Barber" Maglie "shaving" Carl Furillo for the final out of the first game of a weekend series with the Giants, and of Yogi Berra clinging apelike to the body of another faceless Yankee hurler after a final series out.

Other Sports

We were so passionate about baseball, basically, because it had no serious competition from any other sport. Monday-night football and the Super Bowl didn't exist. The Giants were standbys in the National Football League, and the Yankees had a team in the old American Football League, which folded into the NFL in 1955. No one in the neighborhood, however, got very excited about these teams, and my only memories are of listening to the daring running of a diminutive player named Buddy Young. The only problem was he played for the Yankees, and I could never in my heart, even remotely, root for a team so named. The wounds inflicted by the Bronx Bombers have left a mark on my innermost soul, and unlike the stain left there by original sin, which the nuns told us the Sacrament of Baptism removes, this mark is indelible and cannot be removed by any rite.

We had the National Basketball Association and the National Hockey League and college sports, but it was hard to get excited about them by listening to games over the radio or by reading the Daily News. Besides, except for college football (all my friends rooted for the army, clearly one of the greatest teams in the history of the sport—I liked the navy), everyone rooted for the same teams; and so there was nothing to argue about.

Boxing was another exception. We would gather around the radio on a Friday night in the back of Mickey Moonlight's stationery store and listen to Don Dunphy describe with unbridled excitement the exploits of the likes of Marcel Cedan, Willy Pep, and Ezzard Charles, only to have his unflappable "color-man" come on to say, "Now that was not a particularly interesting round." Again, what did make it particularly interesting for me was some unexplainable trait to always seem to root against the grain of the rest of the neighborhood—Tony Zale over Rocky Graziano, Sugar Ray Robinson over Jake LaMotta, and Jersey Joe Walcott over Joe Louis.

We vaguely knew about other sports, like skiing, tennis, and volleyball; but Americans only enjoyed these. We knew a little about bowling because some of our older brothers would set pins for ten cents a game (automatic pin setters have wiped out that noble trade). Golf, however, was a notable exception. We knew a lot about that game, because as soon as we reached the age of roughly twelve, we were ready to become caddies.

Caddying

This was truly the only downside to summer, and there was just no escape. I knew that every summer weekend, at a minimum, I was going to be at the whim and mercy of the most fearsome, dictatorial individual I would ever encounter: the caddy master Matty (Amorasano). What power he exuded as he stood there holding an ever-present clipboard in his bony hands while his beady eyes scanned the inhabitants of the caddy yard at Hampshire Country Club, in Larchmont, New York. I would stand there motionless knowing that only one of two things could possibly save me from being chosen:

1. A thunderstorm! How I would pray for this, especially for a local outburst that would send me scrambling to hitch a ride back home to listen to the Dodgers on the radio, after explaining to my mother how it was raining and lightning at the course (that was always a clincher) or
2. Getting overlooked! This took a lot of ingenuity for someone my size, as it involved hiding under benches or behind trees or going off into the woods to take a leak at an opportune time.

It was fraught with danger of the worst kind; however, as I could successfully manage to dodge a "loop" all morning only to subject myself to the worst imaginable of all nightmares, for at 1:00 p.m. sharp, there would emerge from the doors of the clubhouse a multitude of bodies resplendent in pastel colors: the ladies. And horror of horrors, if their husbands played golf badly enough, they would accompany them.

Imagine my state of mind when I had successfully managed to be avoided all morning, eaten my lunch (usually by 10:00 a.m.), downed several Cokes, and was just beginning to feel safe only to hear at 2:00 p.m., when most of the other "loopers" were happily heading home, "Semenza, take Mr. and Mrs. Fudder on the tenth tee!"

Actually, there was a third possibility. I could manage to get a member pissed off enough to not only "pop" me (no tip in caddy talk) but to complain to the caddy master. This could result in a temporary holiday—oops, I mean suspension. This was something I, of course, wouldn't do on purpose—I had some pride—but sometimes it was just unavoidable. A typical scenario, culminating in a suspension, might go something like this:

> **Matty**: SEMENZA! Mr. Messinger just told me you lost twelve balls on him. What the XZ?/&* is going on?
> **Me**: But, sir, (murmured with feigned respect), he sliced five of them into the swamp off the first tee and shot a 102.
> **Matty**: That's not too bad.
> **Me**: But he ran out of balls on the sixth hole.
> **Matty**: Unprintable!

The only two good things about looping were Mondays and the Annual Caddy Day. The caddies got to play golf on Mondays, and even though they left the sprinklers on and set up temporary greens, it was great to play member for a day. On Caddy Day, we not only got to play golf but were also allowed into the clubhouse and locker rooms, but not the pool. The members must have been worried that we would piss in the water or infect it with some mysterious marine malady. The highlight of the event, however, was the dinner after which prizes were given out for the various tournaments held during the day and for other dubious honors such as:

> Caddy of the Year!
> Best Rookie Caddy!
> Best Sand Trap Raker!
> Most Improved Caddy!

I never won an award as they didn't have a category for Worst Caddy of the Year.

The evening would close with a few stumbling, insincere words from Matty after which he would be presented with a "surprise gift" from his caddies. This was financed through a campaign, which always started a few weeks before the dinner whereby a percentage of your meager caddy fee was "withheld" by the caddy master; this was my first exposure to extortion.

Summer Evenings

Sitting on the front steps of our porch late on a hot summer evening and listening to the sounds of the street will always linger on my memory, like the soft breeze that would bring us some relief from the humid night. But what I will never forget are the aromas that those breezes brought and one in particular: freshly-baked bread—ahhhhhhh! We were literally surrounded by several bakeries, and if I would have to choose only one food I could have for the rest of eternity, it would be Italian bread (macaroni would be a very close second). We would go to one of the bakeries and bring home several loaves of hot bread, which we would devour with heaps of real butter, not margarine, or fresh dough that my mother would dip into a pot of boiling hot oil to make pizza-frite.

Summer nights meant going to Columbus School to watch the Twilight League and root for our heroes to hit a home run over the left field fence and into Saccone's Lemon Ice Stand. I don't know how he did it, but Mr. Saccone had the magic lemon ice touch, and people would line up at his small stand as he scooped it out with a huge ladle into a soft paper squeeze cup. I have tried all of the "Italian" ices that later came onto the market, but nothing ever came close to his.

The Twilight League had some outstanding players, including my cousin Louis; and my particular favorites were Joe Merc (Mercurio), Nello Amori, Otto Miller, Freddie Cianciulli, Fred Todaro, Sal Scalfani and Seeley Burigo, and someone named Tutti. He was older than most of the other players and had the slowest windup I have ever seen, equaled only by the lack of velocity on his hard stuff, as he tried to sneak it past Joe Merc—no way.

Hudson Park

Summers meant swimming at Hudson Park! Everything about this beach was special to us; and I can still vividly remember climbing to the top of a small hill on the path, which led to the entrance, and seeing the sun glistening off the cool, beautiful (to me at least) waters of Long Island Sound. As we walked happily along, we would always stop to feed the goldfish in a small pond that was just off the burning pavement and next to a sign that read, "Do not feed the fish." We would pass by an outdoor concert stand, and in my entire lifetime in New Rochelle, I was to never see a concert performed there.

We would then gaze to the right at a small covered veranda that overlooked the water. This was a favorite spot of my father and, in my later years, of my wife, Marie, and me, especially during the hot summer months of 1957 where we sat . . . and sat . . . and sat . . . waiting for the arrival, albeit very late, of our firstborn child, Barbara.

Marie Vaccaro and I were wed in Blessed Sacrament Church on June 17, 1956, a week after my graduation from Iona College. The Vaccaro family was from the town of Bonefro, Italy, in the province of Campobasso, which labeled them as "bunnies."

Her father, Luigi, as he told me at least a thousand times, had "come to this country in 1910" to work in the coalmines of "Union-a-town" (Pennsylvania), leaving his wife, Pasqualina, and five children—Nicolas, Angelo, John, Frank, and Ann—in Italy. The courage and determination of our immigrant ancestors never cease to amaze me; it is unbelievable how they were willing to leave all their loved ones and travel over an ocean to a country where they could not speak the language, and work countless hours for minimal wages. He returned to Italy where he was drafted into the Italian infantry on the outbreak of World War I, the so-called "war to end all wars." He would tell me marvelous stories of fighting on the Austrian front and of crawling into a trench at night to try to get some rest, only to have to go scrambling out to another one when a conversation would begin—in German—that was another kind of war.

In the late 1920s, he came back to America with his eldest son, Nicolas, to make enough money to send for the rest of the family. They came over later, and the family settled in New Rochelle, where Marie was born (on July 8, 1934, one month to the day following my birth), forever labeling her as "the Med-e-con baby." They were living on Main Street at that time, right around the corner from PSA, where many of the "bunnies" lived and which housed their social club: the Bunny Club, of course. PSA? Marie would always claim she was not from PSA, as most of her young life was spent on Seventeen St. Joseph's Street, where her father bought a home. However, the true facts were indisputably confirmed at my daughter Barbara's marriage in response to a question raised by Joel Ratner, one of our closest friends from Stamford, Connecticut. He asked Uncle Columbus (you'll meet him) where Marie was from; and he, without a moment's hesitation, replied, "She's a Bunny from **P**ig **S**hit **A**lley."

I loved her family; and when her mother and father passed on, at ages eighty-eight and ninety-three, respectively, I mourned them as I had my own parents.

Back to Hudson Park. As we passed through the turnstile into the beach, we had to make a decision—do we go to the old beach, the new beach, the pier, or the rocks? We never chose the old beach as the water was icky, especially at low tide. We never sat on the sand at the new beach, but we would love to swim out to the "float," and one of the proudest days of our lives was when we were finally able to make it at high tide. We generally didn't sit on the pier as this was where our older brothers and sisters were with their sweethearts—ugh! This left us with the rocks, and they were great as the water off them was the clearest in the park, and we could jump off them to our heart's content.

Two things were always certain, however:

1. We would never get a locker—only the Americans used them. We did, however, like to wash the sand off our feet in a small foot shower that was just past the front entrance.
2. I would never take off my T-shirt even in the water—my nickname wasn't Chesty for nothing.

Just to the left of the lockers, however, was our favorite spot in the whole park: the candy shack. Few things could compare with the taste of the frozen Milky Ways and other treats sold at this little slice of heaven.

After a long day at the beach, we would head out to wait either for the bus to take us home or for my father to pick us up. We would wait in a small shelter on the pier in front of the bus stop, nursing our sunburned backs while throwing rocks at the crabs and into the muddy water bed to get the "piss clams" to spout up a small stream of water (or piss). If we were lucky, we would spot an occasional water rat scurrying by beneath the old structure.

We would look out at the boats in the harbor, including two of the most famous "legends" of Hudson Park: the party fishing boat, the Klondike, and a Chinese junk that sat in the harbor and that no one I knew ever saw under sail.

Next to the pier was a Greek restaurant; and although I do not recall ever eating there, I do remember, in my teen years, meeting the owner's beautiful daughter in the movies and—that's another story.

Boat rentals were also available, and one day my cousin Ronnie and I decided to rent a rowboat to go fishing; the only problem was neither of us had actually ever rowed a boat before, and as it was a very windy day, we kept getting blown under the pier. It was much more fun being on top of the pier.

We might also venture over to the parking area to watch the men fishing off the concrete platforms for flounders, begalls, black fish, or anything else that happened to be swimming by. I particularly remember one character who would draw an audience around him as he would put his head way back and, as everyone stood wide-eyed, dangle a live, "wiggly killy" over his open mouth, which he would then drop and swallow whole.

I love to fish and have a hundred fish stories, but that's another book. One of my favorites, however, took place on the night of Marie's New Rochelle High

School senior prom. I was all decked out in a tuxedo and she in a beautiful gown, and as it was too early to go to the affair, we decided to go to Hudson Park and look at the sunset. It was a beautiful night, and all the usual fishermen were there, when all of a sudden, they started catching some very big fish. I had never seen an event like this before, and I rushed to get my ever-ready fishing gear from the car trunk and join in the catch. I started pulling in fish without even baiting the hook; it was a pool of some unknown (at least to me) species of fish that had made a fatal mistake by swimming past this pier at the wrong time. It is not difficult to imagine Marie's reaction when I held up my oily catch for her inspection!

The prom turned out to be a great success, in spite of its smelly beginning, and ended the next morning when we followed a long-standing tradition by driving out to Jones Beach in Long Island, New York, with several of our friends, to lie on the sand and watch the sunrise. I always wondered what the rental establishment must have thought when they cleaned my tuxedo.

The Hudson Park parking area was a favorite place for Marie and me to go during our courting years in order to watch the nocturnal "submarine races." Another favorite spot was a parking lot off the Shore Road just over the Bronx line. This was actually one of the "lovers' lane" sites where, in the late 1970s, David Berkowitz, the "Son of Sam" serial killer, murdered two of his victims.

Every week, however, we would have to forsake Hudson Park for Wilson Pool in the neighboring town of Pelham. They had an offer we couldn't refuse: free Friday morning admission. One of the best parts of the day was walking to the pool as we had to go through a dark tunnel that ran beneath the Hutchinson River Parkway. In later life, as I was to read the amazing adventures of Bilbo Baggins and his first encounter with the odious creature lurking in a murky underground river (and from whom he was to take the ring that formed the centerpiece of the Tolkien Lord of the Rings trilogy), I was reminded of the stream that flowed through this tunnel and of the bats that hovered overhead. That was fun!

Oakland Pool and Playland

If I had to pick the most favorite days of the summer and of my childhood, which would be a tough choice, it would have to be those that began by waking up on a bright, sunny morning and rushing downstairs to wake up Ronnie to plan our trip to "paradise": Oakland Pool and Rye Playland. We would have to get an early start to make the long drive to Rye. My father would generally wake us up, not by calling our names but by whistling a little tune that sounded similar to the melody played on a Rinso White radio commercial. I never forgot that little "annoying ditty" and was to use it to wake my own children and grandchildren, much to their chagrin. My father, who was always up before the crack of dawn, would get everything together, including his "famous" pepper-and-egg sandwiches, which he would wrap in aluminum foil to keep them moist and warm. We would get into the car and patiently sit as he went through his usual ritual: adjusting the rearview mirror, arranging his hat, tapping a cigarette on his Chesterfield case several times, lighting up the cigarette, asking if we had everything including our handkerchiefs (this is something he asked me every day right up until I got married), and so on.

Oakland Pool was situated on Long Island Sound and just across a small bay from Playland. It was classy and beautiful! They didn't just have lockers to store our clothes in, they had an entire room for us to use, as well as private showers and wringers to help dry our wet bathing suits. The options were endless—we could settle on either the grass, concrete, or sand areas; use the swings and slides in the playground or play basketball or shuffleboard; or swim in the sound (they had a small concrete stairway that led to the water, and it was always a little scary to jump into the dark, cold water; but we had to do it as it was part of the experience) or in the huge saltwater pool.

But best of all, we could jump off the diving boards. There were three of them, ranging from a run-of-the-mill variety up to one as high as the bathhouse; our favorite was the one in between, a ten-footer. That may not seem like much until you actually got out at the end of the board and looked down. It looked endless, especially if you were only eight years old. We never actually did dive off that board but would get up enough courage to just run off the end of it and head for the water feet first. What a sense of exhilaration we experienced as we plunged breathlessly through the air and of triumph when we splashed into the warm, salty waters. They would never let us dive off the high board, and we were grateful for that because we would have certainly felt challenged to attempt it if the opportunity were presented.

Visiting Oakland Pool was indeed a full day in itself, but the best was yet to come! As the afternoon wore on, Ronnie and I would begin to stare off across the bay to the most wondrous site in the world: the Ferris wheels and roller coasters, which rose out of the far shore—Playland. This was truly a magical land for us (and continued to be a place I was to take my children and grandchildren to), and if you don't believe me, watch the boardwalk scenes filmed there for the movie Big.

Playland had so much to offer us: rides, miniature golf, batting cages, rental boats, food, and, best of all, the boardwalk games to play. I was especially adept at a game where I would race a rabbit against other contestants by rolling a small rubber ball into a slot, which would move it at either a slow, medium, or fast pace, depending on which slot it rolled into. My trick was to time the first roll to coincide with the moment just before the official start of the race and to never—never—look up to see where my rabbit stood in the race. This would cause me to lose precious seconds and spell certain defeat. I was unbeatable and in later years was so proficient at this game that they often wouldn't let me play after winning a handful of stuffed animals.

I was also good at a game I was to never see again—one that required you to have a monkey climb up a tree by turning a small wheel. As my father would often say, "There's a trick to every trade," and I had figured out the trick to this game: turn the wheel at a steady pace as it would fall back if you changed speeds.

I was a true student of these games and would study several previous contests before I would plunk down my nickel to look for any possible advantage, however slight. For example, I would see if any of the numbered positions were consistent winners, as this generally meant they offered some mechanical advantage. I told you I won a lot.

The game, however, for which I will always be remembered for by my family is "getting the softball into the tilted basket." I was, and still am, the "master." My skill came at a great price—I had lost all my money playing this game at the Danbury Fair, which was held every fall in Danbury, Connecticut. Unfortunately, the fairgrounds have since been replaced by a shopping mall. I didn't even have money left to buy a sausage-and-pepper wedge. I vowed never to lose consistently again and constructed a simulated game on a pole in my backyard and practiced endlessly until I had perfected a way of putting a backspin on the ball to keep it from bouncing out of the basket. I then scoured every amusement park, carnival, and bazaar looking for this game and savoring the prizes I would always win.

Back to Playland and the rides! They were awesome. There was the famous Dragon Coaster, which had an enormous drop; the high-speed Airplane Coaster; the Whip; Laugh-in-the-Dark; the Old Mill, which was said to contain black widow spiders; 1000 and 1 mirrors; the Flying Wing, the bumper cars; the Steeplechase, which only our older brothers got to ride; and so on.

The most unique amusement to be experienced, however, was the Magic Carpet Ride, and I have never seen another that could offer as much for your money, not even at Disneyland or Six Flags. It was so much more than just a ride. We had to first wind our way through a maze of strange rooms, including one that was tilted causing us to struggle to maintain our balance, in order to reach a large "fun house." This contained a variety of unusual and never-to-be-seen-again diversions, and although we never saw any human operators, the amusements always started up as soon as we were near or on them. There was a bus that would take us on a bumpy journey and a room with little round circles on the floor that would spin around requiring us to hold on to Tarzan-like ropes that hung from the ceiling. But best of all, there was a large cylinder in the middle of the room that we would sit on and that would spin around at an ever-increasing speed, causing the centrifugal force to send us careening off into the outer limits. The trick was to sit near the middle of the cylinder and to never sit on the small metal objects; these would cause you to get a small, but effective, shock. I always imagined the Wizard of Oz controlling the switches to these electric jolts from his hiding place behind a small curtain.

We could, and did, literally spend hours in the fun house until it was time to ride the Magic Carpet. This was the only way out, and there was no way back in, unless you were willing to use up more of your valuable tickets. We sat at the top of a large chute that propelled us over a bumpy ride down to the exit—it was truly magic. This amusement, like many of the others at Playland, was to burn down, never to be duplicated, and Oakland Pool was replaced with condos—what a shame.

Other Trips

My father also took us to other amusement parks, including Coney Island in Brooklyn, where we got to ride on the famous Steeplechase; but we were, unfortunately, too young for the Parachute ride. He never would take us to Palisades Park, in New Jersey, which became a favorite with my family (and which has since been replaced by high-rise apartments), as he would never drive that far even for, as he would say, "a crate of chickens."

There were a number of other memorable trips Ronnie and I would make with my father each summer. He would take us to the Bronx Zoo and to the Aquarium in Battery Park (no longer there) and for a ride on the Staten Island Ferry (we actually never got off—we just cruised past the Statue of Liberty and over to the Staten Island dock and back) and best of all to Ebbets Field (bow your head). We would ride the train and subways all the way to Brooklyn—talk about a father. Amazingly, he would never actually come into the stadium as he hated crowds. He did, however, have a way to cope with one on those rare occasions when he was actually in a crowd. He wouldn't leave until everyone else had cleared out as he was in no rush to go anyplace or to do anything. He would sit in a park outside of Ebbets Field and smoke his Chesterfields, patiently waiting all day for us to come out. He knew how much the Dodgers meant to me; and although Ronnie was a Yankee fan, he enjoyed the trips, especially when the Dodgers, on rare occasions, lost. I can still see the images in my mind:

> Pee Wee (Reese) effortlessly fielding a grounder, Jackie (Robinson) rounding third base with his spikes flashing in the midday sun, Roy (Campanella) and Gil (Hodges) hitting gigantic home runs over the center field wall, Duke (Snider) hitting a rocket onto Bedford Avenue, Billy (Cox) backhanding a shot down the third base line and "counting the stitches" on the ball before rifling a throw to first to beat the runner by a step, Skoonj (Carl Furillo) playing a rebound off the right field wall and whirling to throw someone out at home, Don (Newcombe) firing a fastball past a batter, Burt (Shotten) sitting in the dugout in his street clothes, the Dodger symphony blaring away, Hilda Chester banging her cast-iron frying pan with a ladle and ringing her cowbells, and Happy Felton hosting the knothole gang.

But getting back to the endless summer, although a lot of our time was consumed by our infatuation with the game played by the "boys of summer," most of our energies went into playing our own "games of summer."

Chapter 4
The Games of Summer

Our games were not ordered from a Sears catalogue, purchased over the Internet, or bought off a shelf at Toys R Us. They were created from our own imaginations and the raw materials that surrounded us—just about anything could be turned into or used for a game: a clothespin, broomstick, inner tube, telephone pole, wall, chestnut, shoestring, pea, can, sidewalk, any kind of wheels, and so on.

Clothespins and Broomsticks

Now what can you really do with a clothespin? Well, you could, and we did, combine it with an old broomstick and organize the first—last and only, to my knowledge—"clothespin league."

We could have simply played stickball with a broomstick and a rubber ball, but we didn't really have an available street. The main streets, like Union and Washington Avenues, were too busy with cars and trucks speeding by; and the side streets, like Third, were either too short or hemmed in on both sides by houses (ah, but Third Street had many other uses, which I will get to).

But we did have my backyard, which was a natural clothespin league playing field:

.home plate that was placed in front of the back side of our stucco house, against which foul tips could harmlessly carom,

.low-lying fences that surrounded the playing field (a field comprised of "native grown" weeds many of which were gathered up and used by my mother to brew mysterious concoctions to treat a myriad of maladies), whose measurements favored neither a right—nor a left-handed hitter:

.fifty feet down the foul lines, marked by the clothesline pole in left and Charlie Rose's shack in right, and

.sixty feet to the power alleys in deepest center to the fence that separated our yard from the Acocella family

An official clothespin had to consist of only wood, with no metal attachments. It not only took a lot of determination and skill to solidly hit one of these wooden butterflies as it fluttered toward the plate, but also uncanny ability to catch one as it zigzagged down from the sky.

We were truly committed to our love for this game—from the early spring training tryouts, to the signing of the "reserve clause" contracts (no free agency in those years), to the actual game, and, best of all, to the postseason honors.

The season of 1948 is typical (as taken from my original "square-deal composition book" in which the official records of every season were recorded for posterity):

BATTING AVERAGES:

B. Semenza (me—although I was right-handed, I was forced to bat left-handed)	.405
R. Semenza (cousin Ronnie)	.385
K. Libertino	.150
B. Williams	.150
A. Gentile (the Flea)	.135

Homeruns:

B. Semenza	39
R. Semenza	36

Pitching:

B. Williams	W—6; L—2
B. Semenza	W—5; L—3
A. Gentile	W—2; L—3

No Hit Games:
B. Semenza—June 10, 1948 (two days after my birthday)
B. Williams—June 22, 1948
K. Libertino (Kenny Lib)—June 23, 1948*

Most Valuable Player—R. Semenza (I was robbed)

* This entry in the book is truly embarrassing, as Kenny Lib not only threw a no-hitter that day but a shutout as well—the only one ever accomplished in the history of the league. It was also the first clothespin game he had ever played—talk about beginner's luck!

Joe Pugliese also played in the league, but he must have failed to make the 1948 spring cut.

Here are pictures of Ronnie and me (at the top), and Joe and Billy (on the bottom) taken in the beautiful backyard setting; my father had better things to do with his life than worry about landscaping. As he often said, "Why worry about it [meaning anything other than eating]? It will still be here long after I'm dead and buried."

Inner Tubes

Inner tubes were not easy to come by and were eagerly searched for; this generally required a trip to the dumps, where my friend's father worked. Actually, trying to avoid being spotted by him was the most exciting part of the trip. If we were caught, he would shout in Italian for us to "vatin a cas," namely, to go back home. This was usually accompanied by other colorful ethnic encouragements, like "ba fan goul," "bastia animal," or "I breaka your face," to name a few; but the inner tube was worth the risk.

In addition to the more conventional uses of a tube for sledding on in the winter and floating on in the summer, they were mainly coveted for their use as the main ingredient used in the construction of a "rubber gun." These "guns" were made from three basic raw materials, namely, a board, a clothespin (that again?), and the strips cut from the inner tube. The strips were wrapped around the barrel (the board) in order to secure the trigger (the clothespin). Other strips were used as the ammunition. One end of another strip was placed on the front of the barrel and stretched over its top to load the trigger. All you had to do then was to take aim at the intended target and push down on the trigger.

This gun, which was considered harmless to humans, was deadly in hunting crickets, mosquitoes, flies, cockroaches, and other small game. I got particular pleasure in using it to bounce a "bullet" off a dog's butt, as I considered dogs to be natural enemies (and still do) and thus fair game. They knew this, of course, and were hard to find, except for Red Hollis's dog—it would find you! He (or she, as we never got close enough to determine its true sex or even its real name) was a big scraggly red mutt of unknown birthright. Although there was no known record of anyone being bitten, his (or her) reputation was enough to send us scurrying for cover if it chose to wander within fifty yards of where we were. It did, however, fear one human being: my Uncle Louie, who would sit on our front porch and make "catlike" noises if the dog approached our house. It would trot down Union Avenue with the sidewalk all to itself, but as it approached our house, it would meekly scamper to the other side of the street even if Uncle Louie wasn't there.

More fearsome, however, was Leo "the Chicken Market" man's dog, who was kept chained in an alleyway next to Mickey Moonlight's stationery store. We would get a perverse pleasure out of watching some unsuspecting soul accidentally brush against the steel gate to that alleyway and then hear them scream with unbridled terror as Leo's dog came charging at them with a bark that was more effective on the digestive system than X-lax. He, or she, was always brought to a jarring halt just short of the gate by a chain that at one time might have been used to hold the anchor to the Titanic. We always wondered, but fortunately never found out, what that dog would have done if it ever got loose. It was just unthinkable. I am convinced, however, that one of its offspring was the inspiration behind the Cujo movie.

These early experiences must have nurtured my life-long fear and distrust of dogs; we never got along. It is conceivable; however, that word might have spread in the "dog community" about the fact that I was directly responsible for the premature deaths, albeit accidental, of two of our family dogs. One of them met his (or her) unfortunate demise after I convinced my parents that I was old enough to lead it around the neighborhood on a leash—wrong! It broke free of my grasp, whereupon it ran into the street and—well, you know the rest. Although Charlie still claims he was the one who let go of the leash, I don't remember it that way—and it is my book. Anyway, we both agree on the poor dog's fate. The other one, which belonged to my Uncle Columbus, met the Grim Reaper after I accidentally let it out of our cellar, whereupon it ran out into the street and—well, you know the rest.

I did, however, love cats; and Ronnie and I each had one, at least for a short time. His black-and-white cat was named Lucky—but that it wasn't, as it only got to live out one of its proverbial nine lives. Unfortunately, Ronnie forgot to take it in one cold night and—well, you know the rest. My cat's name was Gray Gray; it was beautiful and began my love of cats, especially gray ones—from Jasmine who was our pet during most of the years we lived in Stamford, Connecticut,—to Figaro who, together with Mookie were the furry "boys" of our son, Robert and his wife, Susan,—to several cats that my daughter Barbara and son-in-law Tim were to own, including their first one, Tasha.

There was one dog that I did grow to love: their dog, Tippy. Although she was a very obedient and gentle mongrel, whenever they came to visit us, I would invoke my "unbreakable rule": "all dogs in the garage or basement." During one particular visit, however, they pleaded with the "Grinch" to let "Max" come into the warm living room from the damp basement, and I reluctantly agreed. Tippy was very excited as she wagged her tail, pranced all around the room, squatted in from of the TV set, and pissed on the carpet.

There were, believe it or not, other dogs that I truly loved: those that I read about in the pages of books written by Albert Payson Terhune. He wrote numerous books; but the ones I enjoyed were those that were written about collies, including my favorite, Lad. The original book on Lad was written in 1919, and a movie was made in 1962 loosely based on several episodes in the book. It is interesting to note that two of the characters in the film were played by Carroll O'Connor—who, of course, played Archie on All in the Family—and Angela

Cartwright, who was in the Sound of Music and many other movies and TV shows. I was thrilled one day to actually discover Mr. Terhune's home—Sunnybank, in New Jersey—and to have an opportunity to tour the grounds. I guess I enjoyed his books so much because I knew that none of the dogs could jump out of the pages of the book and bite me in the ass.

Incidentally, dogs weren't the only ones to blindly run into the street. I did likewise on a dare from Billy Williams—only to be hit by a car. Fortunately, it was on the most protected part of my body: my ass. I can still vividly remember rolling down the street like a barrel, which I actually resembled, and coming to rest in the gutter. I quickly got up, ran into the house, and hid under my bed. This was not exactly the most pleasant place to be, as although my mother had many wonderful traits, cleaning was not one of them. The driver of the car followed me into the house, and he and my mother were able to convince me to leave my dusty hiding place to make certain I was not seriously hurt—only my pride was.

Back to Gray Gray—it just disappeared one day! I was to search endlessly for it and always suspected that it was stolen. Why would any animal want to run away from me?

Telephone Poles and Walls

The telephone pole at the corner of Union Avenue and Third Street was ideal for playing hide-and-go-seek and for what was, without a doubt, the roughest game we ever played: Johnny-ride-the-pony (also referred to as Buck-buck-how-many-fingers-up).

Self-appointed captains, who would "choose" to decide the order in which they would pick their players, formed teams of four to five kids. Most of the preambles to our games involved "choosing," and this never bothered anyone because we all knew what our respective abilities and limitations were. I knew I would never get picked first in any game that involved speed, agility, etc.; and thus, I generally made sure I was always the captain!

Once the teams were picked, the captains would again choose to see which team would get to "ride the pony" first. The losing team got to be the "pony." One member of the pony was used as a "pillow"—need I go further as to what my usual role was? He (for obvious reasons, girls were never allowed to be "pillows") would stand with his back against the telephone pole, or a wall, while a team member would bend at the waist and wrap his arms around his waist. The other players would similarly wrap their arms around the waist of the teammate in front of them, thereby forming a human chain—the pony. Each member was thus bent over with his face in very close proximity to the rear end of his teammate. Farting at this point was a definite no-no.

The pony team would then secretly pick a number from one to ten, which the pillow was honor bound to honestly reveal at the appropriate time. The other team would then line up about twenty feet down the sidewalk, and each member would run as fast as he could and use his hands to spring off the backside of the pony, namely, the person at the end of the chain; jump as high as was humanly possible; and, most importantly, land as hard as he could somewhere on the pony. Each player would similarly follow with the object being, obviously, to break any part of the chain. If it broke, they got to ride the pony again. If any of the riders touched the ground with any part of their body, their team got to be the pony. If all the riders landed safely, one member of the pony had to shout out, usually in short painful gasps, "Buck, buck, how many fingers up?" One of the riders would yell out a number, and if he guessed correctly, his team got to ride the pony again. If he chose the wrong number, however, the roles were reversed. It's not too hard to imagine the retaliatory mood of someone who has had his so-called friends land on his back several times when he finally gets the opportunity to ride the pony.

Chestnuts and Shoestrings

Of all the joys of my early years, one of my most vivid memories is of standing under the huge chestnut tree just past the entrance to the cemetery, which was just off Second Street. It was, of course, a place we never ventured into at night, but during a windy fall day, it was the place to be! We would anxiously scour the ground below the spreading limbs searching for the prickly small balls, which the squirrels hadn't discovered, and gleefully gather all we could find, which generally weren't very many, as it was one of the few chestnut trees to be found in the West. We would carefully open the protective shells to hopefully reveal a beautiful shiny brown-and-cream-colored chestnut. We would then hurry home to prepare them for the only purpose, as far as we were concerned, for which God had created them—no, not to be sold by a street vendor for roasting and eating, but to be strung from a shoestring to be proudly paraded around the neighborhood to seek out others similarly showcasing their prized possessions. There was no one more revered and respected on the streets than someone who possessed a chestnut, which had survived numerous battles and achieved an "old age" measured by the number of its victories.

How did one engage an enemy chestnut in mortal combat? You would simply approach someone and ask them how old their chestnut was, and they were honor bound to tell the truth. A decision then had to be made as to whether or not you wanted to engage it in a "fight to death." There was a lot to be considered. If you had an old chestnut, you didn't want to risk it against a potentially stronger contender, and so you generally looked around for a weaker foe. If you had a new chestnut, you would challenge anyone as you had nothing to lose.

If it were agreed that a battle would ensue, the combatants would choose to see who would go first. If you won, the opponent would dangle his chestnut by the shoestring; and you would wait until it stood absolutely still, take dead aim, and strike it with your chestnut. You would continue to do this until either of you broke the enemy's chestnut or, heavens forbid, you missed; then they got to hit your prized possession. It was indeed a very sad moment when a hairpin crack first appeared on your chestnut; you knew then that the future course of events was irreversible. It was just a matter of time before it would split into tiny pieces. Although its demise was inevitable, you would continue to do battle even though only a tiny bit of your brave combatant hung desperately to the string as the encounter raged on to its conclusion.

But if you won! You would proudly add another year to your chestnut's age and then make another momentous decision. You would thoroughly examine it to assess its overall condition and then decide to either fight again or officially retire it. In reality, few chestnuts ever got the opportunity to retire as it was considered honorable to fight on and to eventually die with dignity on the field of combat.

There were a lot of theories as to how you could improve the strength of your chestnut, the favorite being to soak it in vinegar and leave it in the icebox over night. What's an icebox? You will hear about them later.

Peas

These had to be surreptitiously removed from a box in your mother's kitchen cabinet (they were never missed). An individual pea would be very carefully placed into your mouth, as you certainly didn't want to swallow a hard raw one, and then expertly shot out through a "pea shooter" at some predetermined target. The shooter could actually be "store bought" or made from a hollow weed, the best of which grew along "Bergeough pond," which, although geographically was not in the West, was considered by all to be part of its general territorial domain.

Peashooters must be outlawed by now. They were the perfect concealed weapon as it could easily be hidden someplace on your body or just kept in your pocket. If you were truly daring and willing to risk it all, you could bring it to school and shoot "spitballs" at your friends (best not to annoy any enemies in class). These missiles were made by taking any common piece of paper and rolling a small wad of it around in your mouth until it was the right size and consistency. Ugh!

Cans

The main reason for eating the contents of a can, as everyone knew, was to make it available for playing "kick the can." Any small can would do, and the only preparation required was to wash it out thoroughly and remove the label. The can would be placed in the middle of a large circle called home, which was chalk drawn in the middle of the street (yep, Third Street). The chalk didn't even have to be bought as we could use the inside of some old plasterboard lying around at the dumps. One player was chosen to be "it," and all the others would scamper off to hide. The secret of selecting a hiding place was not only to avoid being found but, more importantly, to also allow you to be able to quickly scamper out, if discovered, in a hell-bent race to reach what was, for that moment, the center of the universe: the can. These hiding spots were ingenious: the top (but never under) of cars, under dimly lit hallway stairs, on fire escapes, in a tree, under a pile of leaves, etc.

It was up to the it to not only find each player, but to also plan the search with computer-like precision as the it could never search too far from home, as on finding another player the it would have to race him or her back home. If the it got there first, the other player was "imprisoned" in the circle. If the it was beaten back to the circle, however, the other player would kick the can, which freed any captured inhabitants, sending them back into hiding where the it had to start finding them all over again!

It is not difficult to imagine the sense of power one enjoyed as they raced ahead of the it toward that beautiful can to send it spiraling down the street with a perfectly timed kick—and all to the encouraged shouts of the soon-to-be-released inmates. It is equally not difficult to imagine the feelings of the it as he or she chased after the rattling can while lip-syncing silent words of hate and revenge. I experienced such feelings many times; as you must have guessed by now, I was not particularly fleet of foot.

Sidewalks

A myriad of games could be invented on a sidewalk, and one of our favorites was "ring-o-leave-e-o." Home had to be large enough to hold about a dozen players, and an ideal place was generally a steel door that led to the cellar of a grocery store or bakery. Again, Third Street had the best location—usually in front of Cassone's bakery, which was owned by Bobeep's family (you'll hear more about him). As in the other games, the it had to seek out the other players and, on finding them, race back to home in order to imprison them on the steel door. If the discovered player beat the it back to home, he or she would release all the captured players by shouting, "Ring-a-leave-e-o."

I have just described the more conventional way in which this game was played. In our version, the captured players would join their hands to form a protective chain inside the perimeter of the door, and if the it reached the home first, he or she could keep all the players imprisoned only by smashing through the chain and onto the door. I was good at this.

Wheels

Another reason for a trip to the dumps was to search for one of the most sought-after commodities in the neighborhood: wheels from a discarded baby carriage. These became the main ingredient to construct one of the most desired possessions in our small world: a wagon. The fun that could be had with a wagon was endless, from just showing it off to entering into a race on Third Street (which had to be temporarily suspended when Georgie Williams broke his leg after running into a rope stretched across the "race course" by my brother Charlie and another accomplice), to using it to haul all sorts of items (especially for the World War II "paper or can drives"), and so on.

An equally valuable "antique" were an old pair of skate wheels. These were combined with a board (generally a two by six), a wooden box, a bunch of nails, and some paint to make a wondrous, albeit very noisy, mode of transportation: a scooter. Everyone would make one, generally in the spring, and proudly display it to their friends.

Rubber Balls

A few things just had to be store bought, however, like a small rubber ball for ten cents, but what a marvelous return was made on that investment. A ball could be used for an infinite variety of pleasurable pastimes, for example:

- Handball—All you needed was a wall or a sidewalk, and the latter was favored in our neighborhood. It could be played with two or four players. Each player had a square to protect, and the object was to hit the ball with the palm of your hand (close fists were not allowed) so that it landed into your opponents' square. They then had to hit it back to your square after no more than one bounce, and if they failed, you got a point. Sounds tame? Hardly! These games were fiercely competitive and demanded quick reflexes, intense concentration, and a willingness to dive, if need be, onto the pavement to return a well-placed shot.

- Stoopball—Again, this was played with either two or four players. A small "ball field" was set up consisting of a "stoop," namely, a concrete step on a friendly stairway, and boundaries marked off in the street. The player who was "up" would throw the ball against the edge of the step, and it was up to the opponent(s) to catch the ball before it bounced. One bounce counted as a single, two a double, three a triple, and beyond that a home run. A ball that was hit beyond the farthest boundary was also a home run. An out was made when the ball was caught on the fly and each side got three outs. The best player always played the infield, or the position closest to the batter, and this required both quick reflexes and good hands. I got to play the outfield a lot.
- Boxball—Undoubtedly our favorite game. It was played with rules similar to baseball but only within the infield bases. Again, this game was adopted to fit in with our environment as we could easily find room to play the game on some side street, generally in front of Bobeep's bakery on Third Street (where else?). Each team had five or six players, consisting of a pitcher, four infielders, and a catcher. (The latter could be eliminated, and it was up to the pitcher to cover home plate.) The key positions were the pitcher and third base. The player handling the "hot corner" had to have catlike reactions and be able to guard against shots down the line, which invariably resulted in a home run. Billy Williams was undoubtedly the best third baseman in the neighborhood. The slowest player was always put on second base as the wall to the bakery backed him up. Guess who always got to play second base? I could, however, play the bounces off the bakery wall as well as Carl Furillo handled the angles off the right field wall at Ebbetts Field. The pitcher delivered the ball on one bounce, and the batter had to hit it with his hand so as to have it bounce at least once in the infield. The "Sandy Koufax" of our neighborhood was Johnny Santacroce, better known as Snake. He was a southpaw and endowed with very large hands, which he would deftly wrap around the little ball causing it to curve, stop, and even back up. He also had an infuriating habit of placing his hands on his hips, leaning backward and letting out a loud laugh as you swung helplessly at his assortment of junk. This made him virtually impossible to hit. He also had an arm like Johnny Unitas and could throw an accurate bullet or a long bomb to his favorite receiver,

Billy Williams (who else), which would travel the length of the Third Street football field, which ran between two well-placed telephone poles. It didn't matter if he was throwing a real football or the homemade version concocted from a milk carton; he was unstoppable.

Trading Cards

Anyone looking back at their childhood has to endure visions of dollar signs dancing in their eyes, as they think of the Mickey Mantle, Willie Mays, and Duke Snider cards, which they either "flipped," "tossed" or "traded away," or were tossed out in the garbage during one of their mothers' spring cleanups! Well, some things are better than money (I guess), and these cards brought us endless hours of pleasure as we enjoyed the various games we invented with them:

- Flipping (or matching)—The object of this game was to simply have your opponent flip an agreed-on number of cards onto the pavement and then try to match all the "heads" or "tails" by flipping an equal number of your cards. For example, if you agreed to chance ten cards and your opponent flipped eight heads (picture-side up) and two tails (picture-side down), you would have to flip eight heads and two tails to win his or her ten cards. If you flipped any other combination, you lost all your ten cards. I was a master at this game! It must have had something to do with my low center of gravity. I would spread my legs far apart (although chubby, I was agile) so that I could limit the number of rotations the card would make on its route to the pavement to about two. By holding the card in my hand in a heads or tails position, I could predict with almost absolute certainty the position it would ultimately come to rest at on the pavement. I was unbeatable.
- Tossing—This game involved having your opponent toss a chosen number of cards against a wall from about twenty feet. You would then have to toss a similar number of cards and would get to keep any of your opponent's cards on which yours landed. He or she, of course, kept any of your cards that missed. I wasn't very good at this game as I was not able to use any of my physical attributes to gain an advantage, and I was terrible at estimating how far the card would travel, especially if I had to factor in wind currents.

Obviously, even if these cards had survived our childhood, their value would have been questionable considering the abuse they endured during these games (wishful thinking?).

Carnival Games

The idea to set up a carnival game usually came to me toward the middle of the summer when I was beginning to get just a little bored with everything else. I would love making all the necessary arrangements to set up a game, which generally required two milk boxes ("borrowed" from Mr. Caruso's pile just outside the back door to his grocery store) and a wide board ("borrowed" from the pile just outside the back door to the plywood factory off Second Street). The board would be placed between the milk boxes and house everything needed for the game.

The game would generally be set up in front of my house and open to anyone who happened to be passing by. The basic idea was to have some sort of games of chance that they could attempt for a small fee. If he or she should win, they would have their choice of a myriad of prizes, generally something I found lying around in the attic and which I didn't want anyway. However, one of the prizes always offered were comic books. This was another one of the many ways I managed to dispose of all those now valuable Batman and Superman editions I had collected.

My favorite game was to "try to get the penny into a whiskey glass immersed in water and sitting at the bottom of a pickle jar." I have no idea who invented this game or what it was actually called, but it was challenging! There were all sorts of theories as to how best to win at this game. Some favored placing the penny into the slot in the jar cap at a peculiar angle and giving it a "little English" to send it "herky-jerky" on its way to the whiskey glass while others claimed the "straight down" method was best. Some insisted on playing with the cap off; and this depended on the house rules established by the game operator, namely me, and, more importantly, on the track record of the bettor.

In addition to the games of chance, I might also have a "flea market" where items could be purchased outright, as well as a lemonade stand on the side. These were especially useful to offset my losses, should someone have had a lucky streak at the games.

As my father would always say, "All things come to an end . . . good and bad." Summer was one of those good things that had to end; however we had all "the other seasons" to enjoy.

Chapter 5
The Other Seasons

Fall

Back To School

Back to school—ugh! Actually, it was fun, at least for the first couple of days. All our new notebooks and pencils were bought at Mickey Moonlight's, and the first markings in the books were made with the utmost care and neatness, which quickly reverted to an unintelligible scribble after the first few lessons. I never could perfect those ridiculous round circles or the other exercises, which were guaranteed by "the Palmer method" to improve your penmanship. My circles always came out looking like eggs.

If my writing ability was (and still is) horrible, it was far exceeded by my inability to draw (except for a talent I developed during my teens for drawing my favorite cartoon character, Bugs Bunny, which I perfected whiling away my summers as an attendant in the woman's locker room at Glen Island Park; but that's another story). I would look forward to the few hours we would have to spend each week on art with utmost dread. I hated it. I will forever remember, however, one particular assignment where we were required to draw a typical fall scene, and I created what I thought was a masterpiece. All the elements were there: open fields and winding roads, bundled stacks of dried corn husks, pumpkins growing wild in the fields, a rambling picket fence, and, of course, a cat! Beautiful! In my mind, I could clearly see all the details of this idyllic landscape; however, something got lost in transferring these images from my mind, through my body, into my right hand, and onto a sketch pad. Somehow, the pumpkins came out looking like tiny spaceships, the winding road appeared to drift off into the sky, and the cat perched precariously right on top of one of the sharp fence pickets. When the teacher saw it, she was so flabbergasted at my rendering that she sent me down to the first grade to display my "art" to that class. I still cannot believe that a nun, or anyone else, could have been so insensitive to my feelings; but even they weren't perfect, I guess. Someone else might have been scarred for life by this embarrassing episode, but as a little fat boy who blatantly rooted for the Brooklyn Bums in the West, I was impervious to any slings and arrows that life could possibly throw my way. I marched straight down to that classroom and displayed my drawing to a rousing round of applause; they loved it. What do nuns know about true art!

I had written the description of my art without having actually seen the famous work for over fifty years, when I discovered it in an old file that was lying around the house. I cannot believe how accurate my memory of that drawing was. See for yourself.

The events that I did thoroughly enjoy, however, were the plays that the school would put on, as I loved being on stage and becoming the center of attention. I generally was chosen to play Santa Claus in the annual Christmas pageant (surprise!), but my most famous role was that of the "Rt. Rev. Bishop," presiding at "Major Tom Thumb's Wedding" in the St. Joseph's School Players' 1942 production of Little Women. Following is a photo of the "wedding," as well as the program from the performance, which were sent to me by the beautiful "bride," Ann Fontanarosa (Gibbons). Although for some inexplicable reason, I was not named in the cast of characters; that's me with the big hat on. I can still remember how difficult it was to keep it balanced on my head. Joe Pugliese (of "clothespin league" fame) is the "best man" to my right.

ST. JOSEPH'S SCHOOL PLAYERS

— PRESENT —

"LITTLE WOMEN"

From The Novel By
LOUISA M. ALCOTT

Music By
GEOFFREY O'HARA

— and —

OUR LITTLE ONES PRESENT

"MAJOR TOM THUMB'S WEDDING"

SUNDAY, MONDAY, TUESDAY, MAY 10, 11, 12, 1942

Eight-Fifteen O'clock

School Auditorium

By special arrangement with Samuel French

CHARACTERS

Jo	Catherine Bartucca
Meg	Angelina Gaita
Beth	Theresa Ferrara
Amy	Margaret Santasurio
Mr. March (their father)	Louis Bernabi
Mrs. March "Marmee" (their mother)	Ada Comi
Aunt March (their aunt)	Theresa Mucci
Hannah (their maid)	Frances Valenti
Theodore Lawrence "Laurie"	Louis Mangano
Professor Bhaer (a tutor)	Anthony Damore
John Brooke (Laurie's tutor)	Frank Da Silva
Fred Vaughan (a neighbor)	Herman Ret

NEIGHBORS

Sallie Gardenier	Rose Guido
Irene Gardenier	Mary Sabia
Mary Gardenier	Amelia Cosentina
Joan Gardenier	Angeline Santacroce
Julia Gardenier	Mary Sergi
David Ralston	Anthony DaSilva
Tom Billings	Angelo Masdarano
George Smith	William Cappellini

ALL AMERICAN CHORUS

K. Carino, F. Marciano, P. Casome, A. Guglielmo, V. Margioti, J. Villamagna, S. La Forte, F. Ciazzo, F. Generosa, C. Fontanarosa, P. Valenti, S. Manzi, M. Calocchio, A. De Rosa, P. Agresta, M. Sabia, A. Da Silva, M. Mandarano, W. Cappellino, R. Guido, A. Cosentino, A. Santacroce, M. Sergi, H. Ret.

MAJOR TOM THUMB'S WEDDING

Rt. Rev. Bishop, *Presiding*

Miss Jennie (June Bride)	Ann Fontanarosa
Major Tom Thumb	Anthony Storino
Maid of Honor	Adeline Boggi
Best Man	Joseph Pugliese
Flower Girl	Janet Fontanarosa
Father of Bride	Cania Ferrari
Mother of Bride	Eugenie Gotti
Military Guard	Guests—Ushers

Each of the nuns at St. Joseph's was so unique and gave so much of themselves to us; of course, we couldn't care less. All we prayed for was lunch and the 3:00 p.m. dismissal bell. One of them, however, does deserve special mention: Sister Raymond.

She was the eighth-grade teacher and truly feared by all. She was a stern disciplinarian, and if you were caught doing any of the numerous things she did not approve of, the penalty was swift. While this deterred us a little bit, it never completely stopped us from trying to "get away with something." One episode clearly stands out in my mind: "the fish caper." For some unexplained reason, someone had brought goldfish into the class, and fearing Sister Raymond's discovery, it was decided that we should deposit them in the fountain that graced the front corridor of Columbus School. The specifics are hazy—we did do it and we did get caught—the rest I remember clearly! Sister Raymond lined up the culprits in a neat long row, many of whom were a head taller than she was; rolled up her sleeves; and gave each of us the hardest slap we would ever receive in our lives. I was always convinced, however, that it must have hurt her more than it hurt us because we were each hit only once.

In this day and age, of course, physical punishment is unheard of (I think), and parents and a school board would be "all over the situation." In those times, it was not uncommon (although certainly not a regular occurrence) to get whacked in the face or in the back of the head; but really, how much damage could a nun do, even Sister Raymond? I always knew I deserved the whacks I got, and no one would ever run home to complain to their parents; they would definitely side with the nuns and probably whack you again.

The desks in the classroom were rather unique in that the surface that you wrote on was connected to the seat of the person in front of you—sort of like a cantilever. One of the dangers of this arrangement was that if you were resting your head on the desk and the person in front of you decided to get up, the desk would collapse, sending you, your books, the inkwell, and anything else you might be squiring away on or in the desk crashing to the floor with a very loud bang. This was a common occurrence for Sally Colangelo, whom you will soon meet again, as he had some type of sleeping disorder and was often the victim of the student in front of him who forgot to wake him up before leaving their seat.

Another anomaly of these desks was the fact that your feet were in very close proximity to the rear end of the classmate in front of you. Sister Raymond—who was relentless in her determination to have us pass the "regents" examinations, which we were required to take in those days—would have us come to class an hour earlier each day to prepare for them. She would not only "drill" the information into our reluctant brains but during a "mock examination" would impose a "no hands up" rule, which meant that no one could raise their hands during the "dry run" to ask a question or for any other reason. I was sitting behind a girl (modesty forbids me from revealing her name), and she kept waving her hand to try to get Sister's attention; she, of course, completely ignored this obvious violation of her immovable rule. As I sat there trying to figure out the answers to the questions on the test, I suddenly began to get a very warm sensation in my feet that was not entirely unpleasant until I realized that the girl in front of me was pissing on them. Obviously, she was raising her hand to request permission to go to the "lavatory" (we couldn't call them bathrooms—why?). Even in those days, I was never at a loss for words, and I quickly jumped up and shouted, "Sister, it's raining in here," and then added, "It's a good thing I wore my rubbers."

Several of my schoolmates went on to very successful careers, including Vinny Grillo, who became a professional golfer; Pat Dorme who had a very successful career in the business world; Johnny DeMaz (DeMasi) who excelled as an insurance salesman; and Sal Candido who, with his brother, formed a company that distributed business machines. Sal Candido—who would have guessed? He was undeniably one of the roughest, toughest characters to ever have roamed the West, and the stories of him are legendary. The one that symbolizes him best, however, is the tale of his having been bitten by a dog, only to return the favor.

He lived on Fourth Street where I went one day to help him paint his family's apartment. As I started to move the furniture out of the way, Sal stopped me and said, "What are you doing that for? Just paint around the chairs and the pictures; my father will never notice."

I should have known that Sal would be a success. One of the assignments we were given was to memorize a poem, which we would have to recite before the class. I chose what is still one of my favorite poems, "Fog," by Carl Sanburg. It went:

> The fog comes on little cat feet. It sits looking over harbor and city on silent haunches and then moves on.

For some reason, Sister Raymond thought I should have selected something a little longer. I would, however, remember that poem my entire life and have been able to rationalize my selection of those few simple lines, not as an adolescent quick fix to a school assignment but as a testimony to the beauty of the simplicity of a few well-chosen but vividly descriptive words. I wish I could have convinced her of that as she chased me around the room and ushered me back to my seat.

But Sal—he picked "O Captain! My Captain!" and we all sat mesmerized as he flawlessly recited that entire poem. Funny how certain moments in your life stay with you all your days. In reminiscing about that day with Sal and his wife at a memorial service for Grace Grosso, held at the Boys Club during the summer of 2001, I was amazed to hear her say he still recites that poem to his grandchildren . . . and I can still recite the "Fog" to mine! One last word about "my" poem—it recently appeared in The Best Loved Poems of Jacqueline Kennedy Onassis; again, what do nuns know of true art?

And then there was Sammy (Fish) Daniele; you will soon hear about his antics on the basketball court. During my many return visits to Cancro's Funeral Home, I would invariable meet Fish, and he never changed. He would greet me with a warm hug and talk in his characteristic quick manner, reminiscing about the old days and bringing me up-to-date on our old buddies.

I was probably the only one in the class who had a set of encyclopedias, and he would always ask to borrow them for a report we would have to prepare. I would generally resist his request, as I was afraid he would just copy the information out of the book; and the trail would lead back to me. On one occasion, however, he convinced me that he would rework the information so that Sister Raymond would never know he had taken it from an encyclopedia rather than reading a whole book, which, of course, he was supposed to do. I was truly proud of him as he stood in front of the class and read a stirring rendition of Custer's Last Stand until he concluded his wonderful essay with the words, "For further information, see Sitting Bull." My cover was blown!

The eight years I spent at St. Joseph's are fraught with so many wonderful memories, especially of the many friends with whom I shared them. These memories are clouded, however, by thoughts of those who left us so early in their lives: Lilly Luiso, Frank (Chi Chi) DeLeo, Joe (Dee Dee) Tedesco, and Paul Amato and Ralph DeRosa, whom you will soon meet.

I have also been saddened by the 2006 passing of my dear boyhood friends: Billy Williams, Sal Candido, Sally Colangelo, and Jimmy "Big Head" Denicola.

Following is a picture of the sixth-grade class; some of them that appear in these pages are (starting from the top row down and going from left to right) the following:

Fourth Row—8th—Joe (DeeDee) Tedesco

Third Row—2nd—Johnnie (Snake) Santacroce
           4th—Me
           5th—Vinny Grillo
           6th—Paul Amato
           7th—Sammy (Fish) Daniele
           8th—Johnny (DeMaz) DeMasi

Second Row—2st—Sal Candido
             3nd—Lilly Luiso
             10th—Frank (Chi Chi) DeLeo

Although I was never a Boy Scout, I did become a "Saint Joseph's Cadet," as did most of my friends; although it is difficult to see much detail, below is a good photo of the playground and the church in the background, and it also includes Father Aldo Carniato (priest on the left), about whom you will hear later.

Leaves

Fall brought so many other wonderful things to enjoy—like falling leaves. In my later years, although I always marveled at the wonder of this magical change engineered by Mother Nature, it was always dampened somewhat by the fact that I would have to rake, bundle, and cart these multicolored beauties off to the local dump. We never had to rake leaves on Union Avenue; the leaves from the few trees near our house simply got squashed by the passing cars and buses.

However, the "rich" people, who lived near the Pelham line or to our north, had leaves, which someone would rake into neat large piles for us to jump into. There was something mysteriously unique about diving into one of these mounds. They could be covering an open manhole to a waiting sewer, having at their center a huge pile of rocks, or, even worse, sheltering a pile of dog shit. Most of the times, they were just leaves, and we would fearlessly jump into the middle of the pile and fling them at each other until our arms grew too heavy, or the "rakee" would shout or charge out at us from the dark recesses of his Tudor-styled home. To this day, I always equate a pile of leaves with wealth!

Football

As I have mentioned, the favorite team of the neighborhood was the army. They were great as all the good players from the other colleges were off fighting World War II. They had Mr. Inside (Doc Blanchard) and Mr. Outside (Glen Davis), and they were awesome. Of course, I rooted for the navy, who always seem to lose. Again, I had to root for the underdog; besides, I liked their uniforms. Although I was never to go into the armed forces, I would have definitely chosen the navy; I liked their uniforms.

We had our own brand of football, which was naturally played on Third Street. Before we could actually save enough to buy a real pigskin, we played with milk cartons stuffed with newspaper, which you had better catch, especially if it was aiming toward your head.

The Warrens

I loved to play tackle football. My size made me a first-round draft pick whenever we chose sides for a game. My reputation spread, along with my girth, and I was flattered to be asked to play with the best team around—the Warrens—so named as most of their players came from Warren Street. They were great, especially their captain, quarterback, traveling secretary, etc.: Big Head (Jimmy Denicola). Most of our games were played on Sundays, and I would go to Mass wearing a long overcoat to hide the football gear I had on underneath. I just couldn't wait to get onto the field. I don't remember us ever losing, but I vividly recall one memorable tie game, which was played at the Isaac E. Young High School field. The school was designed as though it were a castle, with torrents, towers, and tunnels that wound their way beneath the huge superstructure—it was beautiful.

On this particular day, we were playing against a team of colored guys, who not only had a full complement of players (we only had about eight that day), but also an entourage of sideline support—it was scary. I was playing at the guard position on offense, and on the first play of the game, the defensive player grabbed my shoulder guards and gave me a swift kick between my legs; boy, did that hurt. After my eyes stopped rolling around in my skull, I turned to see their entire team on top of Big Head. I wasn't too concerned as they only seemed to be hitting him on the most impregnable part of his body: his head. It was clear to me that it would be every man for himself that day, and so I sought to make peace with the guy across the line from me. On the next play from scrimmage, I simply stepped aside and let him rush by me to beat up on Big Head—or so he thought. As he sped past me, I hit him square in the nose with a well-placed elbow and sent a gush of blood splattering across his confused face. I figured I was dead; unbelievably, however, he just looked at me in disbelief and offered a truce—whew! Big Head really lived up to his name that day, and we were truly proud of him as he kept picking himself off the ground and leading us on to a scoreless tie.

We were concerned, however, about what might happen to us after the game and kept a low profile as we made our way to one of the tunnels to change back into our street clothes. Big Head kept warning us not to say or do anything, which might set off a massacre, and we were certainly heeding his advice. The colored guys, however, weren't buying into our quiet demeanor and were just waiting for a chink in our armor; it came. One of them went over to our running back—Sally (Colangelo), a terrific athlete when he was awake—and suddenly slapped him in the face as he shouted, "And what the hell are you smiling at?" To which Sally honestly replied, "I'm not smiling. I always look this way."

Winter

Snowstorms

Winter brought us one of the greatest reasons for being a kid: snowstorms! Can anyone remember something more exciting than waking up on a school-day morning (God forbid, they came on a weekend) and hearing on the radio that school had been cancelled by a major snowstorm!

There are few more pleasurable moments in life than those first few minutes when you got to slip back under your warm blankets and dose off to the thoughts of the wonderful adventures to be enjoyed throughout that now most magical of days. It was even better than waking up on a normal day off from school, such as on a weekend or a holiday, because it was so unexpected. On those days, I would generally crawl under the covers with a flashlight, as I didn't want to wake up Charlie who always slept late (and still does), and let the pages of a book enable me, in my mind, to float down the Mississippi River with Tom Sawyer and Huckleberry Finn, search for treasure with Long John Silver, visit strange, faraway lands with Gulliver, and solve crimes with the Hardy boys. I have never lost this early love for reading.

When I awoke on a snow day, however, there was no time to waste. I would have my usual breakfast—a glass of milk and three Yankee Doodles (they now only come two in a package)—and, best of all, I could really take my time enjoying them. This involved a special ritual whereby I would crush all three of them into a glass of milk, imagining them to be submarines struck by a torpedo, and then spoon them out, being careful to eat the creamy centers first. Whoever claimed I was normal?

Then it was time to get dressed and go out into the winter wonderland. A typical outfit would include a pair of jeans; a Tom Sawyer shirt, which I got every year from Gumma Francis (Capio) (even after I was married); a mackinaw jacket, galoshes; a hat; and gloves. It seems everyone in the family had Gumma Francis as their godmother and her husband, Gumba Dominic, as their godfather. I have no idea why, although they were very religious, and she would go to Mass every morning. They lived on Charles Street and had two sons that I particularly remember—Bruno and Frankie Capio—and you could never meet two more contrasting individuals. It is inconceivable how Bruno could have been the son of so "saintly" a pair of parents; Frankie, on the other hand, was a "laid-back" trumpet player; and, at one time, Marie and I rented rooms on the first-floor apartment of his home on Harold Court, where he lived above us with his wife, Nettie. She was not as easygoing as Frankie and would continually complain about the "noise" our infant daughter, Barbara, would make until we were forced to move out. If there was one thing that Marie would never stand for, it was an attack on her family, and as we were leaving the house, she looked straight in Nettie's eyes and shouted, "You have some nerve complaining about our daughter. Wait until your daughter has children. I hope she has twin boys, and they wreck your house." She did, and they did!

Back to the snowstorm. I would go up to the attic to get my Flexible Flyer sled containing a year's buildup of rust on its rudders and rush out the front door to be greeted by a never-to-be-forgotten sight as Union Avenue had been transformed into Main Street, Bedford Falls (as in the scene from A Wonderful Life—this later became everyone's favorite movie, but I even liked it back then). It all looked and sounded so different; there was a quiet hush over the neighborhood as no cars or buses were rushing by, and all you heard were the sounds of footsteps over freshly falling snow. My love of falling snow has never deserted me; even in my twilight years, when many of my closest lifetime friends are basking in the Florida sun, I am still dreaming of being deep in the woods where I can stop and listen to the wonderful "sounds of silence" that surround me, or on the slopes immersed in that powdery gold.

The idyllic scene on Union Avenue was soon to end, however, as all the kids rushed from their homes with their sleds, searching for asphalt beneath the snow to try to scrape the rust off their runners. Then we all headed to paradise: the Fourth Street hill. Although I was to take up skiing, the greatest love of my life (besides Marie), in my early forties and was to ski some of the most exciting, breathtaking mountains in the world, I could never forget the excitement I experienced as I stood at the top of that hill looking down at the snow-covered pavement.

During major snowstorms, the street was closed to traffic (why?), and everyone was there! We would slide down the street all day and into the evening, being careful not to hit any of the stranded cars parked at the curbs. Someone was also posted at the cross street, Lafayette Avenue, at the bottom of the hill to watch for moving cars as that street was not closed to traffic.

Snowstorms also brought other opportunities to supplement our meager incomes from caddying and shining shoes—shoveling driveways. Snowblowers, of course, did not exist. This involved going to the "rich streets" as no one on Union Avenue and the surrounding area would pay to have snow cleared from their sidewalks, and, in any event, few had driveways. We would generally head to Pelham and begin to size up potential customers. We would look for houses with very small driveways and very old people and would send one of the more "underfed and hungrier-looking" members of our group to the front door (I never got to go) to ask if we could shovel their walk and driveway for a small fee. It generally wasn't worth it—that was hard work.

I will never forget the winter of 1946-47. The snow was unimaginable, and school was closed for several days. We built huge snow forts and tunnels right on Union Avenue, and the snowball fights were legendary. In fact, the book Snow in August—written by one of my favorite authors, Pete Hamill—had this storm as its centerpiece.

Spring

The snow would, of course, always melt, even in 1947; and soon the Baseball Annuals would show up on the magazine racks in Mickey Moonlight's store. This meant it could not be very far away: spring training. There were other things to do in the spring, however, other than scouring every conceivable magazine or newspaper, which had anything to say about my Bums, and to wait for that "day of days" when I could again hear the golden tones of Red Barber, and his sidekick Connie Desmond, announce the first exhibition game. There were, of course, the Clothespin League tryouts and all the street games we loved to play, but you know all about these—and then there was fishing.

Fishing

The greatest thing about having a father who had no lofty ambitions in life was that he was home most of the day and had all the time in the world for us—his "four" boys. Most of my time was spent with Ronnie, as we were closer in age, and it was not very difficult to talk my father into going down to Burgeough pond to fish for "sunnies." All we had to do was to ask. He would send us out to the backyard to dig up some worms (we never bought them), and up into the attic to get our gear. He would never fish himself, however, as this would have required him to get a license; this was unthinkable to him. His greatest worry (and perhaps the only one he ever experienced) was getting snagged by the game warden. He would go on forever warning us about them. "I can't even bait the hook without a license, or even take a fish off the hook," he would caution us.

He would contently sit under a tree, smoke a Chesterfield (after tapping it repeatedly on a small tin case he kept them in), pick up and admire a small bird feather, sip coffee from a red-and-brown thermos, laugh as we caught one small sunny after another and put them in a large pickle jar, and look up at the sky and the trees and the lake and proclaim with a sigh, "Ah . . . this is God's country." Anywhere he was, was God's country for us.

We were to find many other wonderful fishing holes over the years—the twin lakes at New Rochelle High School (we never caught much there, but it was such a beautiful spot), the reservoirs at the end of Webster Avenue (we never caught much there, but they were such beautiful spots)—but then there was Interlaken. After years of pulling out sunnies, we finally hit the big time. Interlaken was actually in Eastchester and was a "private lake" for the use of the residents of a townhouse community. There was a back way into the lake, however; and we would drive down an unpaved road and park the car right on the far shores of this beautiful, clear, and clean lake, which happened to house one of the best kept secrets in the world: an inexhaustible supply of hungry largemouth bass. We would fish for these beauties with "killies," which were small bait fish we would buy from an old gentleman down on the docks of Long Island Sound. That alone was worth the trip; we would get there early in the morning, and if he wasn't there, we would reach into the dark waters and pull up a large mesh cage in which the killies were swimming around. We would scoop them into our bucket with a small can and pay for them by putting the money into a tin box he would leave on the dock for his early morning customers. The bass could not resist these saltwater delicacies. And after catching our limit, Ronnie and I would swim or float on a tube during the heat of the day, listen to the Dodgers on the radio, and eat my father's "trademark" pepper-and-egg sandwiches. Could life ever get any better than this?

Interlaken was eventually turned into a very exclusive housing community, but I was gone from New Rochelle by then. Whenever I happened to be in that area and drove by, I always felt as if all those wealthy people mowing their fine green lawns were trespassing on my memories. My cousin Louis was to later buy a home on Interlaken Avenue, in New Rochelle, New York; and I purchased a town home in a community on a lake in Saratoga Springs, New York. The name of the community? Interlaken!

One last memory of the original Interlaken—my father and my cousin, Johnny DiPippo, had to come to my rescue one fine day as I had driven the car too far into a thicket and got stuck in the mud. As they were pushing my car back to the main road, they kept muttering, "But why was he trying to park in there? The fishing is the other way." Marie and I didn't have an answer for them. (Did I forget to mention that she was with me?)

Donald Vec, whom you will meet later, also loved fishing, and he told us stories about a mystical lake that lay in some far-off place to the north; he called it "Stump Pond" and claimed it was loaded with chain pickerel. He was finally able to convince my father (how, I'll never know) to go there; and on a beautiful Saturday morning, he, my father, Charlie and me got into the car and began our long northward trek. As soon as we pulled away from the curb, my father started in, "Why the deuce are we going all this way to fish when we have all these lakes right near us?" The word deuce was the closest he ever came to a curse word. He was relentless as we drove on in the dark through the winding roads until we mercifully reached the pond as the sun was rising over the murky waters. We could readily see why Donald had christened it "Stump Pond." We found a place at the far end of the pond where an old fellow rented rowboats, and as we were paying him, he asked us where we were from. When we said we were from New Rochelle, he laughed and unbelievably replied, "New Rochelle? Why did you come way up here? I go down there all the time to fish—it's great!" Need I say more? My father never let us live that one down.

Actually, the fishing was terrific, and we hauled in one pickerel after another, just as Donald had claimed. Just look at the string of them, which I am holding.

Although we never took my father there again, it did become one of my favorite places to fish. Joseph Calo Jr. and I loved to go there even after I was married. In fact, we were there when Marie was expecting our first child, and I had to keep rowing back to shore to call her from a pay phone to make sure everything was fine. Joseph could not understand why I kept calling. As he said, "What could you have done if she were having the baby? We were two hours away."

Funny, although we went fishing a thousand times, we never did see a game warden.

Finally, there were places that had no season—they were always there for us—the Boys Club and St. Joseph's Church, simply referred to as the church.

Chapter 6
The Boys Club

The club was situated in the placid green surroundings of Feeney Park, which also housed the library, where the reigning monarch was Miss Schmidt. How imposing she was as we stared up at her while she scrupulously searched the little card tucked away in the back of the book to see if we were late in returning it. One of my greatest fears in life was to forget to bring one back on time. This, of course, resulted in a fine of a penny for each day it was overdue, which I would have to fund from my meager caddy earnings or ask my mother for it. This was something, however, I didn't bring up casually. I had to prepare a plausible excuse as to why the book was overdue, such as "I forgot because of the pressures of homework" (a good one), or I would try to shift the blame to my brother or cousin. I certainly didn't want to lie as this would bring on a worse fate: I would have to confess it on Saturday afternoon. Miss Schmidt did have one other distinguishing feature; we would all wait for her to leave the protective surroundings of the counter and marvel at the size of her legs—they were huge!

Movies

Everyone went to the Boys Club, especially on Friday nights when they held the movies! There was a definite pecking order as to where you sat in the gym during the show. The girls sat in the "orchestra," namely, on metal folding chairs lined up across the gym floor; and the boys in the "balcony," that is in the bleachers to the rear of the gym. The "bigger" or "tougher" you were, the higher you sat in the bleachers. If you were really a "big wheel," you were entitled to sit in the "mezzanine"; that's where Hank Deck (Frank Declemente), the chief honcho of the club; Joe Biff (Bevalaqua) and Sonny Mecca (more about them later); and other "dignitaries" hung out.

For a mere six cents, we could see a "funny picture" (now referred to as a cartoon), a feature-length film, and, best of all, a serial. Of course, we never actually watched the feature, which was just a "filler" between the funny picture and the serial. Everything was in black-and-white and shown from an ancient projector, which sat in the middle of the mezzanine above the gym. Joe Biff generally controlled the projector, but Hank made all the big decisions. If the weather was especially bad, for example, and he wanted to keep us there a little longer, he would have Joe Biff run the movies backward; that was great.

The funny pictures usually featured a Farmer Brown and his assortment of barnyard animals. We rarely got to see Bugs Bunny, Tom and Jerry, Daffy Duck, Mickey Mouse, or the other Disney characters, as these were a special treat.

The main feature was usually a boring love story, which we would ignore. The only time we would pay any attention to the movie was if it was a "war movie" (now referred to as an action film) or a "cowboy picture" (now called a Western).

The serial, however, was something special, and no one ever left before it came on; that's why Hank always put it on last. They were marvelous, continuous episodes that always ended with the hero in the throes of a life-threatening predicament from which there was apparently no escape. He is lying unconscious in the backseat of a runaway stagecoach, which goes careening over the edge of a cliff and is plummeting five hundred feet down to the bottom of a river-swelled canyon! This is the topic of conversation for the entire week, during which time we would argue over the possible methods of escape and generally conclude that there just weren't any. When the serial continued the following Friday, however, somehow . . . somehow the hero manages to escape. There is always an ever-so-slight change in the beginning scenario, which differs from the ending scene, which we had seen the prior week.

The Friday-night movies at the Boys Club were generally considered impregnable, but so was the Maginot Line—and why pay six cents when it was so much more fun to try to sneak in? It did, however, present certain risks, which had to be taken into account, if caught. A number of things could happen, none of which were good, such as the following:

- I could, at best, merely be sent out of the club with a kick in the ass from Joe Biff, or

- Hank Deck could tell my brother who was then honor bound to tell my mother, or
- I could get suspended from the club, which was not an uncommon occurrence for me.

Anyway, the challenge was worth the risks. Infiltration was dependent on having someone inside the gym and could only be accomplished by impeccable timing and uncommon daring. The only possible way in was through a set of doors at the back of the gym, which were accessed through a long dark tunnel. The doors could only be opened from the inside by pressing down on a very squeaky handlebar. Timing was very important—pick the wrong time and the entire gym would hear that squeak! You had to pick just the right moment when you knew the entire assemblage would be in pandemonium, namely, the exact instant the title to the funny picture was flashed.

Mr. Inside (someone small and inconspicuous like Billy Williams) would have to surreptitiously make his way to the door by crawling wormlike down the tunnel ramp or slowly creeping along the wall, silently praying the ever-vigilant Joe Biff or Sonny Mecca would not spot him. The outside crew had to also be on the alert for Sam "the Watchman" (Mistruzzi), who was always scouring the park for who knows what.

Assuming Mr. Inside makes it that far and even manages to open the door at just the right moment, the infiltrators were still faced with seemingly impossible odds. Someone could see a shaft of light from the door opening, or they could be spotted by any one of their "friends" in the bleachers, who would be only too willing to blow their cover and shout out a warning signal to Hank Deck and his boys. There was also a better-than-even chance that at the precise moment of break-in, the projector could jam and the house lights go on!

Believe it or not, on one unforgettable occasion when everything went just right, we did it—Billy Williams, Billy Rose (who was as red as his name implied), and me, Chesty!

We had a myriad of "real" movie houses to choose from in New Rochelle: the RKO, Lowe's and the Trent on Main Street, and the Alden and Orpheum on North Avenue. The highlight at the Trent was a "triple feature" on Saturday afternoon, especially when a raffle was held between the movies for members (which everyone was) of the "young fun club." The words to the club song would flash on the screen, and we would all follow the bouncing ball and sing, "Young fun club, young fun club, young fun club for you and me." I would pray to win one of the prizes: a Red Ryder BB gun; a pair of Red Devil skates, which my brother Charlie did win; or a bike. I never won! It was just as well. I could generally convince my mother and father to get me just about anything except for:

- a bike—Charlie fixed that for me by heading down Second Street, the steepest hill in the West, and crashing into a telephone pole
- a BB gun—for obvious reasons; however, I had my homemade rubber gun, or
- a chemistry set—they were frightened, and probably with good cause, that I would blow up the house.

Movies were special to us during any part of the year, even though we had to pay to see them occasionally. My favorite movies fell into the following categories:

- War movies (World War II, of course)—Bataan, Guadalcanal Diary, Action in the North Atlantic, China, The Sullivan Brothers, and Purple Heart. We were, of course, too young to understand the true horror of the war. It was something that was being fought in some foreign lands, and our images of it were based on the "glorified" scenes depicted on the silver screen in the newsreels and feature-length films—and how we loved them. Although we had to "suffer" through air-raid drills in school, paper drives, food, gasoline, and other rationing and blackouts at night, we believed there was absolutely no way the war could actually touch us in the United States and that it was, of course, inconceivable that we could ever lose any war.
- Horror movies—Anything featuring Frankenstein, Dracula, and, my personal favorite, the Wolf Man (portrayed by Lon Chaney Jr.). I really sympathized with that unfortunate human (?). It wasn't his fault that a "carrier" bit him on the neck just when he didn't happen to have a silver bullet handy. And what about his poor mother (unforgettably played by Maria Ossusupenski—she was actually scarier looking than the Wolf Man), who had to ride her wagon through the nighttime fog of some god-awful town somewhere in Hungary, trying to convince anyone who wasn't scared off that the guy with the hairy face and arms (we never saw the rest of him) and big teeth was a loving son and only got nasty on nights when the moon was full (yea, yea)?
- Cowboy movies—Hopalong Cassidy, Red Ryder and his sidekick, Little Beaver, Gene Autry, Roy Rogers, and Tom Mix.

Some of these movie houses, however, hold other special memories in my mind—how we managed to "sneak in" to them! Although none of them were as daunting as the Friday-night movies at the Boys Club, each presented special obstacles, which had to be cleverly overcome; and we were clever!

- The RKO—Simple! This was best assaulted by chipping in to buy a single ticket, which would be used by one of the more trustworthy members of the group to legitimately enter the theater through the front door. The rest of us would head for a small side alleyway, which led out from an exit door, and the plan was to have our inside man open this door to let us into the theater. This, of course, was not entirely unknown to the theater management, and they would have their ushers stand guard at these vulnerable points of potential illegal entry. They couldn't stand there all day, of course, and this is where Mr. Inside had to summon all the wisdom of his young years to select the most opportune moment to slither over to the exit door and ever so softly "spring the lache"; then all hell would break loose, and it was every man for himself as we would scatter to different sections of the darkened theater to find seats and stare innocently at the screen. There were inevitably some casualties who would be discovered and led out the front door by their "shirt collar." They would either try to sneak in again or head back to the West and wait in front of Mickey Moonlight's store to later hear about the movie from those who were lucky enough to have escaped detection.
- Lowes—This presented a special challenge as the "back door" option was considered nearly impossible. The most vulnerable point, however, was a small rear window in the men's room that stood about five feet or so from the floor. Fortunately, one of the few trees that grew near Main Street stood alongside this window. We could carefully climb up its trunk, crawl out onto a limb, and squirm through that small window, which was opened by an accomplice who had paid his way into the theater; this was always my role, as there was no way I could scale that tree, and even if I could, I would never fit through the window opening.

These methods were obviously very risky, and our highest success rate was on days when a truly special movie was being shown, such as a Walt Disney flick. We would simply wait for the audience to come steaming out after a showing and walk in—backward!

Activities

Back to the Boys Club; it consisted of three levels and held no end of activities to absorb our young minds and bodies. On entering the main entrance, you encountered a bulletin board where current events would be publicized and "inspirational" messages displayed. Billy Williams and I especially liked the one showing a youngster (in a beanie cap, I believe) expressing his gratitude for the opportunity to be a part of the club by proclaiming, "Thanks for the break." We would use this slogan on more than one occasion as he and I were being led out of the club for some minor infraction of the rules, like sneaking into the movies; getting caught in the "senior only" game room; climbing into a second-story window to explore a room that was off-limits to the membership (I never did find out why); or, most serious of all, smoking in the bathroom.

A stairway to the second floor was on the right, and a hallway led to the office. You didn't want to go in there unless you were renewing your membership card; you might run into Mr. Morton S. Furst. I never actually knew what his official position was, except that Hank Deck reported to him in some way. He was a white-haired, meticulously dressed elderly gentleman who would always wear a white suit and shoes as he led us down Main Street during some holiday parade. His only other official duty appeared to be to gently pat our heads as he showed visitors around the club. His disposition, however, completely changed when the visitors were out of sight; and he was then to be avoided at all cost.

Down the hallway from the office was the locker room and showers. I, of course, would never even think about taking off my clothes and actually showering there—no way! I would rather die than have someone see my "chubby" body. I would wear my gym shorts under my clothes and go home all sweaty to shower and change. The main purpose of going into the locker room was to laugh at anyone who did strip and shower.

The junior game room was down at the end of the hall and was where we spent a lot of our time playing pool, Ping-Pong, checkers, and other assorted games.

If you took a left out of the office, it led down two flights of stairs to the gym. A flight of stairs could also be taken up to the balcony, which overlooked the gym floor. The gym is where we spent most of our time playing basketball, dodgeball (one of my favorites), and attending the infamous Friday-night movies, the annual Halloween party, roller-skating parties, boxing events, etc.

The main attraction throughout the winter was the basketball leagues, which we all followed with great interest. My favorite team was the Jeeps; they always had the worst record in the league. I had to root against them, however, when they played the Nabs or the Barons, as my brother Charlie and Cousin Louis played on these respective teams.

A foul-smelling bathroom was off to the side of the gym floor and a small room from which candies were sold at the various "social" events, which the club sponsored.

The balcony over the gym was also one of my favorite places as it had all sorts of boxing gear, including a large medicine ball, a huge punching bag (I would always scrape my knuckles hitting the bag with my bare hands), and a small punching bag used to perfect your timing (I never could quite get the staccato beat down). There were some excellent boxers at the club, and several of them went on to the Golden Gloves. I especially remember Mickey Circelli, whose father was a boxing coach. One of the highlights of the year was the annual boxing tournament held at the club. My favorite part was a free-for-all when everyone in the ring wore one glove and was, best of all, blindfolded. The mayhem that ensued was unbelievable, especially when one of the many characters in the West, Rocco (Zipilli), got in the middle of the action. He sure could take a punch in the head.

The second floor included the model airplane, woodworking and print shops, and the library, senior game room, and the mysterious locked room already referred to. The woodworking shop had all types of saws and other interesting equipment to make an assortment of wood items, and a little alcove where the wood was stored. Although I never successfully made anything, I always enjoyed going into the airplane and woodworking shops—maybe it was the smell of glue?

The library contained a variety of ancient books that no one I knew ever looked at and was used to conduct periodic bingo games. I enjoyed these immensely, especially as candy was given out as prizes. It also contained one of the earliest and strangest TV sets I would ever see; it had a round and very tiny screen. In any event, we spent many enjoyable hours squinting at the black-and-white images of our favorite baseball teams, the Milton Berle Show, Your Show of Shows, Howdy Doody and Buffalo Bob, and so on.

Let me offer a few more words about Hank Deck, Joe Biff, and Sonny Mecca, as I have already mentioned them several times. Hank had one very distinguishing feature: he was never seen without his hat on! As the miniscule few that saw him sneak into church attested to, this was due to the fact that he had only a few wisps of hair on his prematurely balding head.

Joe Biff, his right-hand man, also had a distinguishing feature, besides his emaciated appearance, in that he was never seen without wearing sunglasses (even inside) and sneakers.

Sonny Mecca was something else; he had several distinguishing features. Although he had no official capacity at the club, as far as anyone knew, he was always in the office or at the side of Hank and Joe. He spoke in rapid, cliplike, unintelligible chirps (that's the best I can do to describe it). He was always dressed in a pair of slacks, jacket and shirt, and tie, which he continually straightened while chattering on about something or another; he was rarely silent! The highlight of his year, however, was the talent show held as part of the annual Halloween party, during which the audience would invariably shout in unison for Sonny to get up and sing "Ciribiribin." We would never in our collective lifetimes hear a rendition that would even come close to his performance; it defies description, and I won't even try.

Another highlight of the talent show was an operatic rendition by Mr. Unkeless's (he ran a dry goods store on Union Avenue) overweight daughter, Yvonne; you can imagine the reception this would wrought from our cultured assemblage!

Halloween

Halloween was, as it is now, a day that was eagerly looked forward to each year, even though we had to attend Mass the following morning (as All Saints Day was a Holy Day of Obligation; after all, that's what All Hollows Eve is about). We would plan our costumes for months, and of course, they would be homemade as we would never consider actually buying one from a store. Although I always gave the matter my utmost attention, I would always settle on being a bum, as the baggy clothes were a perfect cover-up for my overweight frame.

There would always be a party at St. Joseph's School, and we would go trick-or-treating early in the evening. The event we would most look forward to, however, was the costume party at the club. What an event! There would be all sorts of games on the stage at the front of the gym; dunking for apples and the cherry-pie eating contests were my favorites. The highlight, however, was the costume parade. How we hoped and prayed our costume would be selected as most original or most something or other, thereby awarding us with one of the cherished prizes. Actually, I did win a prize one year by pulling out a huge checkered handkerchief from my baggy pants and blowing my nose right in front of the judging stand making an outlandish sound with a hidden noisemaker (the fact that Grace Grosso, one of my mother's closest friends, was a judge didn't hurt my chances). The most unforgettable and original costume, however, was clearly the "bushman" outfit. I don't remember who the individual was, but on arriving in Feeney Park without a costume, the culprit improvised by merely removing one of Sam "the Watchman's" cherished bushes and wrapping it around him—was Sam pissed!

In the final analysis, I could never imagine anyone brought up in the West who would harbor anything but the happiest thoughts and memories of the Boys Club. It was truly our second home and did instill in us values we would carry with us all our lives. One of the proudest moments of my life was my induction into the club's Inspirational Hall of Fame. I guess the induction committee had no record on the number of times I was led out of the front door!

Chapter 7
The Church

Altar Boys

St. Joseph's Church—how our lives were entwined with that place of worship. The great ambition of our young lives was to be an "altar boy," and many of us thought, at one time or another, of actually being a priest; that didn't last long, however. Becoming an altar boy meant achieving the seemingly unattainable: learning Latin. The Mass was, of course, celebrated in that ancient language and no one had any idea what was being said, except for those with a missal. For most of the celebrants, of course, it wouldn't have mattered if the Mass were in Latin, English, or any language other than Italian. If you were to exclude the children from St. Joseph's School, who had to go to the 9:00 a.m. Mass every Sunday, 99 percent of the remaining celebrants consisted of women, most of whom wore black dresses, in perpetual mourning for their deceased husbands, and who spoke little or no English. Although Italian men would say, without hesitation, that they were Catholic, it was a rare sight to see many of them in church on Sunday. I don't ever remember seeing my father or Uncle Louie there other than for weddings and funerals. The priests, of course, knew this and would have to give hand signals at these occasions to let the men know when to stand up, sit down, or kneel.

Latin—was that tough—"Adeum que le tificat, youvem tootem meyhem" or something like that! All that mattered was that you could recite the responses at the appropriate time and without hesitation—the faster the better.

In those days, the priest celebrated the Mass with his back to the parishioners and facing the altar, which stood at the top of several marble steps. One of the functions of an altar boy was, for reasons I never understood, to proceed up those steps on the right side of the altar, pick up an enormous book from which the priest prayed, proceed back down the stairs, genuflect at the bottom, and proceed back up the stairs to place the book on the left side of the altar. The trick, of course, was not to trip on the long black cassock you had to wear under your starched white blouse, and I almost never did! Yes, on one occasion as I was proceeding down the steps, I tripped and sent the book flying into the aisle, accompanied by a startled gasp from the few old women in attendance that morning.

One of my favorite duties as an altar boy involved the burning of incense. This was only done on special occasions, for example during Masses for the dead (or as we called them, dead Masses), a novena, or on Good Friday. I enjoyed carrying the incense holder by its long golden chain, lifting the cover so that the priest could add the incense into the burning embers and, best of all, walking around the altar surrounding it with the sweet-smelling aroma of the incense. If you were truly lucky, you could get to do this during a procession around the church; the only problem was you had to do your "thing" while walking in front of the priest—backward! The trick, of course, was not to trip on the long black cassock you had to wear under your starched white blouse, and I almost never did! Yes, on one occasion as I was proceeding backward down the center aisle of the church and during the most solemn part of a Good Friday service, I tripped and sent the incense flying accompanied by a startled gasp from the few old women in attendance that evening.

Father Aldo Carniato

The parish was not in the best of financial health, until arrival of the most unforgettable priest I, or anyone else in the West, would ever meet: Father Aldo Carniato! You either loved him or hated him; there was simply no way you could remain partial. I loved him. We had a special relationship that began when I was serving the seven o'clock Mass for him one morning and noticed there were no ushers in the church to "pass the basket" at the offertory part of the service. When I realized this, I simply walked off the altar and did so myself. Father Carniato was so impressed with my financial ingenuity that I became his favorite altar boy from that day forward. I found the way to his heart: money! His efforts to raise it for the betterment of the parish were legendary and one of the main reasons most people hated him. One of his techniques was to urge the parishioners to make the Offertory a "silent collection," namely, to offer only bills and not any noisy coins. He did succeed, at least in this regard, and remodeled St. Joseph's to make it a truly beautiful church.

He and his little terrier had come to St. Joseph's from a very tough section of the Bronx, and he stayed there for thirty years. He once took me to visit his mother, who lived in a tenement where I believe he was raised, and I remember how very proud she was of him. He had a well-deserved reputation as a no-nonsense priest who got the job done at any cost and who feared no one. The stories of his exploits followed him, particularly the time he presided at the wedding of a well-known Bronx boxer, Tami Mauriello. Tami had a very large family and an even larger following of fans, and as the story goes, the church resembled Madison Square Garden during a title bout. Father Carniato, who was a very imposing figure himself and had a very deep and commanding voice (much like the famous actor Orson Welles), walked onto the altar and threatened to clear the church if the raucous behavior didn't stop; it did.

He ran the parish with an iron fist. In those days, women were required to have their heads covered during the Mass, but he went one better: he required them to wear hats. If some unsuspecting woman was to try to walk into church with just a scarf on her head, he would be lurking in the vestibule with a boxful of the most awful-looking headwear imaginable and would plop one right on their unsuspecting head! An even worst fate could await them if they tried to receive Holy Communion with too much lipstick on; he would give them the body and blood of Jesus Christ, contained in the host, but would first wipe off the lipstick with a well-used handkerchief. I told you he was tough!

My favorite story, however, was the legendary Ash Wednesday episode, and Marie and I were actually there to witness it. For the uninformed, Ash Wednesday signals the beginning of the forty days of Lent preceding Easter Sunday, the most sacred of all Christian holy days. Everyone went to church on that day to have the priest make the sign of the cross on their foreheads with the ashes made from burning the palm left over from the prior Palm Sunday (actually, it just looked like you had forgotten to wash your face). The ashes were meant to remind us of the Bible's indisputable prediction that "dust you were and to dust you will return," and you got to walk around the rest of the day or night proudly displaying this sign of devotion to your faith. A large crowd was assembled in the darkened church waiting for the blessing and dispensation of the ashes to begin. There was a long delay while the church continued to remain in darkness, and everyone began to look around and wonder why the lights weren't being turned on. Suddenly, a large figure moved out of the shadows from the side of the altar and stepped onto the podium. It was hard to tell who it was at first as he was covered with a black cape; it soon became clear who it was: Father Carniato! Again, I can't resist the comparison with Orson Welles as he climbed the pulpit, shaped from a New Bedford whaling ship's bow, to deliver the famous sermon in the film version of Moby Dick, proclaiming that "if God were a fish he'd be a whale." Father Carniato simultaneously ordered the lights to be turned on, and the doors to be locked, and announced that anyone with plans for the evening should forget them! He then proceeded to deliver the most stinging sermon I, or anyone else present that evening, would ever hear. He denounced those who showed up only on Ash Wednesday in their fur coats and fine clothes (they certainly stood out from the black-draped regulars), so that they could publicly display their Catholicism to the world. He chided them for thinking that receiving ashes would atone for not showing up the rest of the year and offered to dump the barrel of ashes on the head of any volunteer who felt this would guarantee entry into the pearly gates—there were no takers. He spoke for over an hour, and when he finished there was a dead, eerie silence in the church, as everyone was justifiably afraid to move or do anything that might, God forbid, single them out. He then asked that the congregation sing a hymn, a cappella. No one opened his or her mouth, except one little old lady (in black of course) who began to screech out some words in Italian. Father Carniato told her to "ashbet," namely to wait, and finally got all of us to join in. There is no doubt in my mind that anyone who was there that night would ever again feel the same about Ash Wednesday.

The Feast

The highlight of the church year, as far as we kids were concerned, was the annual outdoor church bazaar (the "feast") held in the school playground. I still cannot pass up one of these events, and they always evoke memories of the utmost joy I would get if I was fortunate enough to have the pinwheel stop on one of my lucky numbers, seven, fourteen or forty-three, and I could choose a prize, preferable a shiny crusader sword.

There was also, of course, the food: the sausage and peppers, the fried dough, the hot dogs, the custard (now called soft-serve ice cream), and so on. The absolute highlight of the feast was the event held on the final evening when there would be a contest to see who could climb to the top of the "greased pole." It was quite a sight to see young, and some old, men trying to scramble up the pole to the cheers and jeers of the crowd, and to see them slowly slip down just before they reached the flag at the top.

An event never to be forgotten, however, took place on another pole in the playground: the flagpole. A real character, Ascadole, decided he would climb to the top of the pole and jump off! No, he wasn't trying to commit suicide; he had been apparently inspired by the Penguin character from the Batman comics and reasoned that he could simply open the umbrella he brought along and float safely down to the pavement. My brother Charlie actually witnessed this auspicious event and watched as Ascadole placed a ladder against the pole and climbed up. His theory actually worked for about the first ten feet or so into the jump, and then disaster struck as the umbrella collapsed (surprise!), and he landed not so softly on both feet, albeit both his ankles were broken (ouch!).

Another highlight of the church year was the processions held on major feast days, like St. Anthony's, my favorite saint, on June 16. A procession would start at the church and proceed down Washington Avenue to Webster Avenue and up Union Avenue—right past our front porch! The men of the Holy Altar Society would carry a statue of the particular saint whose feast day was being observed, and procession watchers would rush out into the street to pin money onto ribbons that were hung from the statues. Other members of the society would "work the crowd" for collections using beer trays. As you already know, my family spent a lot of time on our front porch, especially my father and Uncle Louie. Neither of them was known for their ability, or desire, to move very fast—except during one of these processions. They would trip over each other while making a beeline to the front door as soon as one of the society men approached the porch to solicit a donation—fat chance!

A fixture at these church events was the "professor" (Angelo Cavalli) and his band. What he lacked in size (he was less than five feet tall), he made up for in enthusiasm, whether he was leading his uniform-clad band up Union Avenue, or conducting a performance in the schoolyard.

Whenever my mother would implore my father to go to church with her, or attend some other religious activity, arguing that he wasn't going to get into heaven, he would always laugh and say, "Mary, I'll take my heaven on earth." He would get a special delight if a salesman selling religious articles should arrive at the front door. If he didn't want to bother with them, he would simply say, "Oh, I don't live here; I'm just the handyman." However, he would generally have them go through their entire sales pitch, showing all their beautiful crucifixes, rosaries, and Bibles, and then say, "They are just beautiful, but we're Jewish."

He did get trapped one night when he unknowingly walked into the kitchen where one of the parish priests was discussing some church society matter with my mother. If he had any inkling that a priest was on the premises, he would have squirreled away someplace with Uncle Louie. The priest was as startled as my father, and on hearing that he was Mary's husband, queried, "Oh, I don't remember ever seeing you in church with your wife?" To which my father responded, "Well, I haven't gotten around to it yet."

If there is a heaven, and I am confident there is, I do not have the slightest doubt that he is there, with my mother by his side, and that he received his fondest wish—to never have to take her shopping on Main Street again; for all eternity.

Confession

Saturday afternoons always meant one thing: Confession! As you had to be at 9:00 a.m. Mass every Sunday and the nuns were there, you had better be prepared to receive Communion. You, of course, could not receive the Communion host if you had a mortal sin on your soul. Venial sins were okay as long as you made an Act of Contrition before receiving Communion; as in my mind I was continually committing venial sins, I would say this right up to the moment the priest put the host onto my tongue (to this day I can't take the sacred host into my hands, which the church later allowed). Mortal sins, however, were a different matter all together and could only be forgiven through Confession! Of course the difference between a venial and a mortal sin was not always crystal clear in my mind, and so I just went to Confession every Saturday just to play it safe (and to this day I cannot go to Communion without going to Confession first, as the difference still eludes me). Of course, if I had an especially good week, I would have to really stretch for a sin, like, "I stole a raisin from the grocery store . . . ah . . . two times."

There was one definite "no-no" to Confession: Father Franco! His confessional was always on the left as you entered the church and the only ones in his line were old women in black dresses (imagine the sins they had to confess?) or unsuspecting strangers. We would be on the lookout for these poor souls who had no idea where that line would lead to, especially if they appeared to have committed some interesting sins. We would wait for them to go into the confessional, close the black curtain, recite the preamble, "Bless me Father, for I have sinned; it has been [however long] since my last confession," and then begin their litany of sins. They might, for example, confess that "I had immoral thoughts twenty-five times"—mistake! This would invariably be followed by an explosive outbreak from behind the screened opening, "What for you do that, you filthya boy!" Father Franco also spoke broken English.

There were other tricks to making your confession with the least amount of personal embarrassment and maximum amount of forgiveness, other than avoiding Father Franco. The best was to try to confess to a visiting priest who didn't speak English. This unfortunately was rare, although I do remember one visiting Chinese priest who always had the longest line waiting outside his confessional. Another secret was to start off with a long list of relatively minor infractions and to quickly slip in a "biggie" when you thought the priest had lost interest.

The Other Guys

Although St. Joseph's was the only Catholic church in the West (I never considered St. Gabriel's at the end of Washington Avenue to be part of the West), Catholicism was certainly not the only religion practiced. We had two other faiths that were especially noteworthy: the "Holy Rollers" and another group whose name I never knew but who were only referred to as the "Save My Soulers".

Diagonally across from our house, at the corner of Union Avenue and Second Street, was a small building, which housed the church of the Holy Rollers. Outside the front door was a huge stone slab (what was that?) that we would sit on during a hot summer evening and listen to the "service" being conducted in the church. It was better than going to the Newport Jazz Festival. Each member of the congregation, consisting only of colored people, was all draped in white garments, and would sing out and wail late into the night. Although we actually never witnessed a ceremony, we were told they would purportedly roll around on the floor in a religious frenzy: the Holy Rollers!

Just up the street from this church, on Second Street, was another small building where other services were held. The leaders of this group were two individuals whom we only referred to as "Mutt and Jeff," as, obviously, one was very tall and the other very short, as were the then famous cartoon characters. They were always dressed in black suits, white shirts, ties, and black shoes with white socks. One of them always carried a small black bag, the contents of which were never revealed to us. I, however, could never get out of my mind the image of Walter Houston, who played the devil, opening his little black bag in the movie The Devil and Daniel Webster and of moths flying out of the bag. They were, of course, the immortal souls of those who had sold out for the pleasures of the world, and as he proclaimed to one of the unhappy takers, "Happiness? I only promised you all that money could buy" (My father loved that line).

"Mutt and Jeff" would parade around the West looking for converts and warning everyone that it was time to "save your souls." We would follow them around singing a little ditty we had composed in their honor, which went "Save my soul on my shoes, it's worn out." We would wait outside their building and watch them spend hours neatly setting up folding chairs for their service. When they were all done, we would sneak in and tip over the last chair in each of the rows causing a domino effect collapse of the "pews." They obviously did not appreciate these antics; however, they not only posed no physical threat to our well-being, but certainly appreciated the tenuous situation under which their "church" was trying to operate. So much for religious freedom!

I have never been accused of having a lack of imagination or organizational skills, and I was at my best in devising new and interesting ways to enjoy our substantial summer leisure time. One of my most ingenious techniques would be the formation of a "club."

Chapter 8
Clubs and Teams

Clubs

The idea for a club could emanate from a movie I had seen, or a magazine story I had read or from something which just seemed to be an interesting theme. If I happened to see a movie on the Crusades, for example, I would start a Crusaders club and outfit the members with capes, swords, and shields—fashioned from old sheets, broomsticks, and the tops of bushels, respectively. Cowboys were, of course, a favorite theme; and we had a number of clubs built around them.

A club always consisted of me, Ronnie and, Billy Williams, at a minimum, and as Ronnie was the youngest, he would generally "volunteer" to act as the guinea pig for some of our more adventurous experiments. For example, I remember one club, which included a herd of wild horses that we had to round up. Unfortunately, he was the only "wild horse" we could find, and we had him run around the yard while we tried to rope him.

Another time, as the Crusaders had to defend their "castle" against an army of marauding "Mongols" from the north, we had to construct a line of defense, including an ingenious catapult which I designed, consisting of a large board which precariously teetered over a huge rock. The plan was to place a large flat rock on one end of the board, which was to be catapulted at the invaders by dropping an even larger rock on the other end of the board. It seemed perfect—on paper. It had to be tested, of course, and Ronnie "agreed" to check it out. We stood there anxiously watching him lift the bigger rock over his head and drop it onto the board. Whoosh! The flat rock on the other end of the board went flying up into the air and we all peered off into the horizon to see just how far it would go. We peered . . . and peered . . . and peered, shielding our eyes from the sun, when we suddenly heard a loud bang, shortly followed by an even louder cry of anguish. The flat rock had unfortunately gone straight up into the air, and then, even faster, following the law of gravity, traveled straight down, landing right on top of Ronnie's head! Oh well, back to the drawing board.

He did get even with us, however by burning down one of our clubhouses—while we were in it! He always claimed the "devil made me do it." We never chose him again for any of our experiments.

Ronnie (dubbed Gabby by Joe Calo) and I were very close and even looked alike. Everyone, of course, took us for brothers and, in my mind, we were. Brothers could not have been any closer than we were to each other. He was a great athlete and went on to be an outstanding basketball player at Archbishop Stepinac High School in White Plains, New York, which we were both to attend. He was selected for the Catholic all-county team, and we all went to the White Plains County Center to watch him play against an all-star team from Philadelphia. Uncle Louie and all of us were so proud of him as he trotted onto the floor and stood next to the tallest, skinniest human being we had ever seen: Wilt (the Stilt) Chamberlain. He was awesome as he single-handedly destroyed our team.

Ronnie and his wife Joan had a daughter, Stephanie, who became an author. Her books were written in the genre of "military romances," and I know that Ronnie must have scratched his "conservative" head many times thinking to himself, "Where did this kid come from?" There is no doubt in my mind that she and I inherited many of the same family genes.

Archbishop Stepinac High School

My years at Stepinac were very memorable, even though I had to take a bus, train, and another bus to get to and from school each day. It was worth it. I was in the first freshman class to attend the new school, which opened in 1948. The movie star, Alan Alda, also attended the school at the same time; however, I never knew him personally, as he hung out with the "artsy-fartsy" types and I with the "jocks."

One of my friends, however, did turn out to be both a professional wrestler and a movie star: Captain Lou Albano. His friendship was not easily won; he didn't think you earned it until he beat the shit out of you—he had a lot of friends. I became his "friend" during an intramural basketball game when I tripped him, and he reacted by ripping off my shirt and shorts and chasing me around the gym with only my jockstrap left to protect me. He then flung me onto the hard court floor and started to choke me before help, in the form of the "shocked" school nurse, finally arrived.

Our friendship, however, was firmly cemented on the football field where I played on offense as a guard, and on defense as a middle linebacker; he was an offensive lineman. Lou was an outstanding football player, was voted to the Westchester all-county team and received a scholarship to the University of Tennessee, where, I believe, he did not last beyond the first semester. During one particular scrimmage, I was on defense and as I also played on offense, I knew what the play would be by just observing the guard, who happened to be Lou. His moves would signal whether it would be a pass, a run through the line or a sweep around the end. This gave me an enormous advantage on defense; as I proceeded to bust up every play and make tackle after tackle. The offensive team was really pissed off at me, as the head coach, Buz Werder, wouldn't end the practice until they "got it right." This finally happened when they carried me off the field with a concussion, which I received from several blows to my chin placed there by Lou's elbow.

Believe it or not, the team doctor was his father—how convenient. The team chaplain, Father Joe McCann had to drive me home, as I was in no condition to take public transportation. I do remember he had a large, beautiful car, and when we arrived at my house, he took me up the stairs and as he stood in the doorway to the kitchen looking down at my mother (he was a big man), calmly said, "Now don't worry Mrs. Semenza, Robert is ok, but—." Before he could get out another word, she had fainted.

I spent about a week at home recovering from my injury, and was greeted as a hero when I returned to school, especially by Lou. Buz called me into his office, and said he would get me into the last few games, especially as I was a senior, and had worked so hard to make the team. I had played on the Junior Varsity team in the previous year and was told I would have to "lose some weight" to make the Varsity. I spent the entire summer not only losing about fifty pounds, but also practicing my blocking skills on a pole in our backyard that the clothesline was attached to. I had wrapped some padding around the bottom of the pole and would put on my shoulder pads and "hit that sucker" all summer long. In fact, I hit it so often that as my father was leaning against it one morning, it toppled over and had to be replaced.

Buz was a man of this word. We traveled to West Point to play a military school one weekend, and it was a very physical game, with several of our players suffering injuries. Suddenly Buz shouted out, as they carried another of our players off the field, "Semenza, go in at middle linebacker." I quickly scrambled around to find my helmet, which I finally located and went running onto the field while trying to get it on. Unfortunately, the play started before I could do so, and it was coming right at me. I shoved the helmet onto my head, without securing the strap, and just dove into the on-coming herd of players and made the stop. As my teammates helped me to my feet, I suddenly realized that I couldn't see, and started to shout out, "I'm blind. I'm blind!" Someone took off my helmet, and my sight was miraculously restored. In my haste, I had put my helmet on backward, and it had slid down over my eyes. Now I was really a legend.

At the end of the game, tempers were flaring on both sides, and the coaches were concerned that there would be a bloody melee. As we stood still listening to a playing of the National Anthem, Father Joe McCann kept quietly urging us to remain calm and not start anything; suddenly, a cannon exploded (after all, it was a military school), and he shouted out, "Jesus Christ, what the hell was that?" So much for remaining calm.

We arrived back in White Plains very late that night, and I called my mother to tell her I was going to stay overnight at the home of my best (high school) friend, John (the Junt) Ryan, who lived in Mamaroneck. Unfortunately, he neglected to inform his mother that I was staying over, and I slept in his sister's bed—no, she wasn't there—I don't remember where she was. As I was very tired from the day's excitement, I soon fell to sleep only to be awakened by the sound of the door slowly opening and of someone tiptoeing into the room. I was terrified; no one, other than the Junt, knew I was in the house and in his sister's bed! I lay there perfectly still, silently praying that whoever it was would go away—not so. I soon became aware of someone breathing very close to the side of my head, which was facing the wall—oh shit! It got even worse as I felt something very warm, and not entirely unpleasant, being squirted into my ear. Fortunately, this seemed to satisfy the intruder who then quietly left the room. I found out in the morning that it was the Junt's mother who had come into her "daughter's room" during the night to put drops into her ear for an infection she had contracted. It is not hard to imagine his mother's reaction the next morning when he told her that I, and not her daughter, was in the bed. We eventually did laugh about it, but I couldn't hear out of that ear for several days.

Believe it or not, his family was really happy to meet me as the Junt had told them I had written a song, "There's Been a Change in Me," which had been recorded by the famous country and western singer Eddie Arnold. I still can't understand why he actually believed it when I told him this fable. I guess I'm more convincing than I think.

My path was to again cross with Lou Albano a few more times. On one occasion, I reluctantly went alone with the Warren's football team for a "rumble" with a "gang" from Mt. Vernon, a neighboring town, for reasons which I have completely forgotten. Actually, this is the only such instance of "gang warfare" that I ever experienced, other than with Fat Danny and his henchmen, which you will soon hear about, as I preferred mediation and other peaceful means to settle disputes. As we strolled into a bar in Mt. Vernon, I peered through the smoke-filled room and could faintly see a frightening sight: a very large figure standing in front of some even larger figures, all of whom were wearing motorcycle jackets. As the smoke cleared a little, I recognized him; thank God, it's Lou Albano. Thanks to me, this turned out to be the luckiest day in the annals of the Warrens, as instead of enduring the worst massacre since Little Big Horn, we wound up partying with our newfound friends.

The last time I saw Lou in person (I caught him on TV and in the movies several times) was on Park Avenue in New York City. I had left my office with several of my partners to have lunch and noticed a large crowd gathered in front of one of the buildings. I made my way to the front of the crowd, and there he was, Lou Albano, all "dressed up" in an outlandish Hawaiian shirt and with his "trademark" rubber bands tied around his beard. He was filming something or other, and he quickly recognized me and shouted out, "Bob, what the f—k are you doing here?" We chatted a little and I explained that I worked up the street as a partner in an accounting firm, which of course paled in comparison with his exploits. I mentioned how I had seen his latest movie, and he blurted out, "I hope the priests at Stepinac didn't see it. I had to say f—k a lot."

By the way, most of the priests at Stepinac drove beautiful cars, including Father Gordon, the Dean of Discipline (just writing about him a half-century later strikes fear in my heart). When I was hitchhiking home one afternoon on Mamaroneck Avenue, a very large black car pulled over, and as I happily opened the door to get into the front seat, the frightful sight of a grinning Father Gordon greeted me. All he said was, "Semenza, you have detention for one week for hitchhiking." This didn't seem too bad to me, as I was usually in detention anyway most of the time. As I stepped away from the car pondering my relative good luck, he gunned the engine, and drove right over my school bag, crushing all my books and all the other contents. That was the last time I used my thumb to get home.

Most of the teachers at Stepinac were priests, which was unusual as generally Brothers did the teaching at Catholic schools. I spent sixteen years in these schools, and several years as an altar boy, and during all that time, I never heard of a case of sexual abuse that has scandalized the Catholic church in recent years.

Below is a picture of me that fall (1951), at my slimmest weight of one hundred and sixty eight, wearing my Stepinac uniform with one of my favorite numbers: forty-three.

Back to the clubs—the best part of starting a club was the building of an obligatory clubhouse in the backyard. This always involved a trip to the plywood factory to pick up spare, and sometimes not-so-spare, pieces of plywood lying around the plant. These trips were always planned around an excursion to the old coal shoot that was located just across the New Haven Railroad (now Metro North) tracks from the factory. I never had any problem recruiting kids to make one of these forays. There was the excitement of locating just the right type of material for our new club, the fun of a slide down the old coal shoot to arrive at the bottom of a black hole with your clothes covered with soot, the lure of the danger of the third rail, and the careful trek on the rails of the bridge over Second Street (there was a safer way to go, but the bridge was much more of a challenge).

The railroad tracks ran past a stretch of land which contained two places that were legendary in the minds of any kid brought up in the West: the hobo woods and the spring water.

Although I was to actually see only a few real hobos, stories of their living in make-shift huts and tunnels dug deep into the ground were enough to make us enter these woods with a great deal of caution and trepidation. They were a great place, however, to roast the potatoes we would "borrow" from someone's garden, as everyone assumed the smoke from the fire was caused by a hobo cooking his supper, and no one would venture into the woods to verify it.

There were few things to compare with the taste of the fresh water that poured from a crop of rocks just below the tracks, especially on a one hundred plus day in the middle of August. I have no idea as to the source of that marvelous spring, but it was undeniably clean, fresh water; it was our Perrier, and, even better, it was free.

The Crusaders

Another one of our favorite sites for a clubhouse was the dirt-floor cellar just beneath the front porch of my house. The only time I saw my father venture into it was to stick a broom handle into a large open pipe, which I believe had something to do with the sewage system. Outside of it being damp and musty, it was a great place for a clubhouse. It became the site of one of the most famous battles the Crusaders were to ever wage, against a ferocious band of "infidels" from a faraway land beyond Second Street and led by an Attila-the-Hun type—fat Danny. He and his boys were not only bigger than us (he was even fatter than me), but overwhelmingly out-numbered us as well, requiring the development of an ingenious and brilliant plan of defense. We knew they could never penetrate the huge door that protected the entrance to our club, but we couldn't afford to stay in there all day. I might miss a meal! I believe it was actually Ronnie who came up with most of the devious portions of our plan, largely taken from bits and pieces of every Crusader movie we had ever seen. After going over the plan in minute detail, we sat and waited for the attack to begin. Soon, an advanced scout knocked on the door and reported a sighting on Washington Avenue, and, after a quick prayer (Crusaders always did that) we all scattered to our assigned positions. The "infidels" began banging on the door to our "fortress," while shouting all manner of obscenities and vivid descriptions of what they were soon going to be doing to us. When the banging proved to be of no avail, they tried to knock down the door by pushing their collective bodies against the ancient wood, and at just the right moment, we obliged them and opened the door. They all came tumbling in and scrambled to try to find us while peering through the darkness, and find us they did! We had a little surprise waiting for them: small jars filled with dirt scooped up from the earthen floor. We flung the dirt into their faces and while they were trying to overcome this further handicap to their ability to see, began striking them with "whips" made from old clotheslines, giving them no choice but to turn and run—perfect! As they scrambled out of the cellar, another harrowing surprise awaited them, as Ronnie and his crew were stationed on the porch just above the door, and began pouring hot water on them from large macaroni pots. We then stormed out of the dark recesses of our fortress and chased them all the way back beyond the bounds of our domain, never to be ever threatened by them again. We celebrated that victory with a Pepsi and Devil Dogs.

On another occasion, as the Crusaders were scouring the neighborhood looking for causes to defend, we were followed by an infidel from below Second Street, Joe Schivone (I think his beautiful sister, Yolanda, was in my class), and he started to mock us and make fun of our attire. As we ignored his taunts, he decided to physically attack me, and he was big enough to take us all on. I was holding a staff in my hand, and as he grabbed it, I simultaneously stuck out my left foot and twisted the staff, sending him sprawling to the ground; again, I was chubby but agile, but now, I was in trouble. Although startled, he quickly got up and came at me a second time—with the same result. He never bothered us again. We celebrated that victory with a Pepsi and Devil Dogs.

On another day, as I was walking alone down Third Street, another of my nemesis, Richie "Skinhead" Contrata, was following me. He was much bigger than I was and loved to pick on me; he was very, very annoying. He was walking closely behind me and kept calling me insulting names, like a "fat f—k," a "lard ass," etc. I quickly turned around and placed a well-timed kick right between his legs, and he slumped to the ground cupping his hands around his wounded area. That was the last time he taunted me, and I celebrated the victory with a Pepsi and Devil Dogs.

Don't mess with the Crusaders!

The Mooseheads

One of my friends, Emerico Colangelie, known simply as Mico, lived at the corner of Union Avenue and First Street, and we formed a club in his basement. On one of our forays to the town dumps, we discovered something that we knew would be perfect for our club: a moosehead. We could not believe our luck, and were at a loss to figure why anyone would throw it away—we were soon to find out.

We carried it back to our lair, hung it on the wall, and decided it looked so great, we would name our club after it: the Mooseheads. As we sat around one evening, we noticed an unusual increase in the normal number of ants crawling around the basement, and we all started to get very itchy. It wasn't long before we discovered the source of the problem—the moosehead—it was crawling with ants. That was the last club Mico's father would ever let us have in his cellar.

The Blood Brothers

Ronnie was also the star of our Boys Club baseball team and of a basketball team I formed: the Blood Brothers. We played in a City league and what we lacked in talent, except for Ronnie, we made up for with ingenuity . . . especially on the part of Johnnie DeMaz (DeMasi), one of the most competitive and talented athletes I was to ever meet. He was simply outstanding in anything he attempted, from baseball, where he was a great pitcher, to golf, where he was shooting in the eighties after only playing a few times, to bowling, to whatever. He was, however, a little too short to really excel at basketball, but he was a master at using the talents he had, and to invent a few others. He was murder "under the boards" and some of his favorite techniques were to either step on an opponent's sneaker, to thwart their jumping ability, or to grab onto the bottom of their gym shorts as they tried to leap for a rebound. This, of course, caused them to forget trying to get the ball, as their hands were otherwise occupied trying to pull their shorts back over their jock straps. I told you he was competitive.

The team also included Pat Dorme, and, I believe, Jimmy Sabia, and Bobby Flynn, and featured Sammy Fish, who seldom was around at the end of the game, as he was generally given an early shower for tripping, fighting, and so on. Sammy Fish lived next door to Johnny DeMaz, however they were never allowed to officially speak with each other because of a long-standing feud between their families. I don't believe they actually knew what the dispute had been about, and if they did, they never told anyone. This was not uncommon among Italian families, who might carry a grudge over from the "old country" for generations, especially if it involved a game of "morra," which I will soon explain.

Fish was not the only one to get kicked out of games. On one particular night, I had been invited to attend a party at the home of the girlfriend of my then best friend, Kentucky (Kenny Carino). I had met her, Marie Vaccaro, while eating a hotdog at the Texas Diner on North Avenue, next to a five-and-dime store, Neiser's, where they both worked. He was tall, good-looking, and smooth talking, and could easily attract the best-looking girls around; and she was no exception. His only problem was me—I was really attracted to Marie and was able to get myself invited to the aforementioned party. The only problem was I had a Blood Brothers game on that particular night, but I promised to be at the house as soon as the game ended, which lasted only a few minutes as I was promptly thrown out for tripping one of the opponents, Johnnie Simmons. I must have been really smitten with Marie, as he was a star tackle on the New Rochelle High School football team, and not someone you wanted to upset. I was out of there before he could get off the floor, took a quick shower, and showed up at the party with my head still wet.

The rest is history—Marie's mother, Pasqualina, clearly favored me over Kentucky. She sat in the living room during the whole party and, although she spoke no English, never missed a trick. When I was dancing with Marie, she would point to me and, without my seeing it, approvingly nod her head up and down; it was "thumbs down" when Kentucky danced with her.

He and I were to go on for several months feuding over which of us were her boyfriend (she loved it), until the climatic night of the St. Patrick's Day dance in the basement hall of St. Joseph's Church. I had been marching in the parade in New York City that day, and arrived at the dance in a manner befitting the purpose for which the day is celebrated—namely, slightly inebriated. After attempting to cut in on their dance, Kentucky invited me outside to discuss the matter. Fortunately, my cousin Ronnie was also there, and, thank God, tagged along. As we were walking past the front steps of the church, the discussion became heated and, without warning, Kentucky hit me in the eye with a sucker punch. I went down in a heap, and Ronnie was on him like a mad dog; Kentucky never had a chance. The rest is still fuzzy, but suffice to say, Marie and I celebrated our fiftieth wedding anniversary in 2006. Kentucky was not invited.

Following is a photo taken in front of Mickey Moonlight's stationery store of Kentucky, Johnny Santacroce and Joe Pugliese who are standing, from left to right, with Billy Williams squatting in between the group.

Incidentally, I had seen Marie at other dances held in the church hall, and in fact I actually "played" in the band on one occasion. Me and two of my closest friends at the time, Babe Branca and Joe Rote (Rotyliano) decided to form a little group; the only problem was that except for Joe, who played a great accordion, Babe and I didn't know how to play any instruments—not to worry.

We simply went up into my attic, where just about anything we could ever need could be found, and quickly discovered the "instruments" we could play: an old waste paper basket, which we covered with some fancy crepe paper, and turned upside down to create a bongo drum and a pair of maracas. We practiced in the attic for days, with Babe on the drum and me on the maracas, and soon felt we were ready for our debut. We were able to convince one of the young priests at St. Joseph's to let us audition for a gig at one of the church dances, and he actually agreed to have us appear—and that we did. I honestly cannot remember if we were any good, as I was too busy seeing who was dancing with Marie. In any event, it was our first and last public appearance.

The Purple Laces

During the summer, it was, of course, too hot to play in the Club, which was not air-conditioned; only the movie houses were so blessed. The highlight of the summer activities at the club was the baseball league. There were some terrific teams in the league, and I particularly remember the Aces—that they were, and they were unbeatable—well, almost. One summer, a miracle was brewing in the West, as a challenger to these perennial champions appeared on the scene—a team called the Purple Laces—how about that name! Their manager was Joe Biff, who scoured the Friday night movies looking for "unsigned" prospects. He came up to me during one of these performances and offered to buy me candy. He never did that, and I was suspicious of his intentions; but, of course, I took him up on it. As I was enjoying a bite into a Baby Ruth, Joe, who rarely said very much to me, brought up the subject of baseball, and said he had heard I was a terrific pitcher. I have no idea where he had gotten that impression, but didn't want to challenge his scouting system and gave him no reason to doubt his information. I just continued eating my Baby Ruth, thinking of all the other goodies to come from playing for Joe's team. I even managed to convince myself that he was right—I am a great pitcher.

I was chosen as the opening day starter—what a thrill! I was surrounded by a wealth of talent, including Cookie and Junior Noberto. Cookie was a tremendous left-handed power hitter who had premature balding hair, which, according to local legend, was caused by a cat having slept on his head one night. The catcher was Lou Tedesci, another outstanding ballplayer. I pitched a few scoreless innings, even though Lou and Joe made innumerable trips to the mound to urge me to "start throwing the hard stuff." Were they kidding? That was my hard stuff! My luck soon ran out; my assortment of slow stuff had thrown them off, but they were getting on to me. I loaded the bases and stood their facing their cleanup hitter, Johnny Gaita. I worked the count full. Joe and Lou called time and again implored me to throw the "high hard one." I reared back and, with all the power of my two-hundred-plus pounds, sent a "bullet" to the plate. I never saw a ball hit that far in the history of the club games, and even my cousin Richie couldn't have caught up to it (you'll hear that story); that was the end of my pitching career. As Joe was leading me to my new position in right field, he kept murmuring, "I just don't understand it. I just don't understand it. Everyone told me you were a great athlete; they said you could punt a football farther than anyone, had the best two-handed set shot in basketball, and were a great pitcher?" I looked at him quizzically and said, "Are you sure they didn't mean my cousin Lou Semenza?" His eyes almost bugged out of their sockets as my words sunk in.

I was able, however, to gain back some respect and was eventually put at second base, my favorite position. Joe Biff found two true pitching gems in Joe Pisch (Piedmont—now Father Joe) and Junior Noberto. We challenged the Aces all season, until it all came down to the final out of the final inning of the final game. We had a one-run lead, but they had the bases loaded. Joe Pisch sent one of his masterful curve balls to the plate, and the hitter sent a slow roller into the infield—more specifically, toward second base. There I was confidently waiting for the ball to reach my glove. I could see it resting in my mitt and thought I would, as Red Barber would say, "count the stitches" before throwing it on to the first baseman in order to savor the moment before joining in the post game celebrations. I still claim it hit a rock. Anyway, it took an unexpected bounce, just as I was having these blissful thoughts, and unbelievably went caroming off my glove and into right field. We lost the game and the championship on that one fatal error (I still think it should have been scored a hit), and I don't believe there was ever more of a "goat" than I was at that moment—even Joe Biff went back to not talking to me.

The Foresters

Charlie, Louis, Ronnie, and I were sponsored for membership into the Court Sons of Italy Chapter of the Forester's International (the "Foresters") by Joe Calo. The secret induction ceremony we had to endure was one of the most painful experiences of my life. I just couldn't keep a straight face as we had to pledge, before the entire membership, that we would support the widows and orphans of those Foresters who died prematurely. Although I appreciated the fact that this was one of the major reasons for forming these associations when our forefathers first came to the new country, this purpose was somehow lost on me as I had witnessed the Morra games and other activities that took place at the Union Avenue clubhouse.

It is almost impossible to describe Morra, as it really had to be seen and heard to be believed, especially as it was played by the Foresters. The idea was simple enough; the players would throw out their hand and shout out a number, getting a point if it agreed with the total number of fingers displayed by both players. Sounds tame—forget it! It was a game of intimidation, as each player would shout out the number in Italian, while sweating profusely and using all sorts of aggressive body language (I told you it was hard to describe). If they won a point by perhaps shouting out "Tuttte grande," which roughly translated meant the "whole world" or the number ten, they would parade around the club holding up the five fingers of their victorious hand while proclaiming their mastery over their opponent; and that was for only one point! When a player won a certain number of points, he was declared to be the "Boss," and his first duty was to appoint an "Underboss." This was not something to be taken lightly, as it was now up to the loser to buy a round of drinks that would be doled out to the thirsty crowd based on the personal selections of the Boss and his Underboss. Now the real fun started, especially if they should decide that the loser could have the entire round and drink it all himself. More often than not, however, the drinks would be divided among their supporters, and a Boss/Underboss might leave someone "dry" every time they had the opportunity. The favor would, of course, be returned when the positions were reversed, and this could, and did, foster a life-long grudge, which many actually brought over to America from their ancestral homes in Italy.

The Sewing Club

As I mentioned earlier, the sewing club met every Wednesday night at the home of one of its members. I don't think anyone actually ever sewed anything; there wasn't time. They were much too busy picking "secret pals," or trying to outdo each other with new tempting and more fattening desserts, and, most importantly, there was just too much to talk about. What could they possibly have talked about for thirty years? Everything! Nothing escaped the sewing club's attention. There wasn't a facet of life in the West (who cared about the rest of the World) that wasn't dissected every Wednesday night over "coffee and." It was absolutely essential not to accidentally stumble into one of these sessions when it was held at our house. This was something to be avoided at all costs unless I was prepared to go through the "third degree."

The sewing club consisted of my mother and Aunt Gertie, Aunt Lena and her sister-in-laws, Feeney (Mangano) and Lulu (DeRosa), Aunt Louise

(Valenti) and her sister-in-law, Florence (Amato), Grace (Grosso), and Cooney (Silo)—what a crew!

Feeney was Uncle Columbus DeRosa's sister and was married to a true character, Charlie Mangano. They had two children, Alma and Buddy. Any wedding that Charlie was invited to was a treat, as after he had "had a few," he would sport an old top hat and cane and perform an unbelievable rendition of Ted Lewis's Me and My Shadow. His performances were temporarily suspended, however, when he suffered a broken leg in a very common accident: he was sitting on the "john" in a bar when the floor gave way and sent him, the toilet, and its contents crashing down to the floor below! If you have to break a leg, that's the way to do it.

Charlie wasn't the only regular to perform at weddings, as Bird Brain's (Petrone) parents usually followed him. The band would strike up a melody and they would gracefully glide along the dance floor, slowly drifting farther and farther apart until they were at opposite ends of the hall. He was very thin and she was a "robust" woman, and as the band went into a drum roll, he would break into a trot, leap high into the air and land right in her outstretched arms. They never missed. Weddings were sure fun in those days; we didn't have to rely on the Bunny Hop, but the tarantella was certainly big.

Lulu was married to Uncle Columbus's brother, Joe and had two daughters, Angela and Rita. Lulu was the last member of this august group to pass on to that "sewing club in the sky".

I was a special favorite of Aunt Louise, and although she was not actually our aunt, she, and her husband, "Uncle Joe" were loved by us as any true relative. They, with their children, Jerome and Pauline, lived on St. John's Place in a second floor apartment above Florence. I loved to go to their house, especially to see something she always had—a canary—and to eat her never-to-be-duplicated rice pudding.

Florence and her husband Paul had three children, Joyce (who suffered from polio), Robert and Paul "Junior," my classmate and one of my closest friends through grammar and high school.

Paul Amato—how I miss him. He was brilliant and I would have never passed high school "trig" if he hadn't spent nights tutoring me. He loved life and all that went with it, and I can still picture him flamboyantly puffing on a cigarette and turning up the car radio volume on a Frank Sinatra record. He went into the army and teamed up with my cousin Ralph in Japan—that country has never been the same. He moved to Chicago (there could not have been a better fit), and I looked him up on one of my many business trips to the Windy City. What a visit—as best as I can remember. It began with dinner, during which we had a few drinks, after which we proceeded to a pool hall, where we had a few more drinks. I, who was not only terrible at the game of pool but who, even at that early hour of the evening, could hardly stand, beat all comers. We then stumbled on to visit, what seemed to be, every bar in Chicago, and to be personally entertained by, what seemed to be, every bar owner in the city. On leaving each of these establishments, Paul and I, and each of the owners, would continue on to the next place. As the sun was rising over Lake Michigan, our entourage was being treated to a private performance by a belly dancer, with a quart of scotch and a neat bundle of one hundred single dollar bills in front of each of us, provided, as best as I can remember, by the owner of the club. The scotch was for us; the bills were for the dancer. From there, I went directly to work, where I spent the entire day behind closed doors—"in conference."

Paul told me during that visit that the doctor's had warned him that his "life style" had affected his health (surprise!), and that he would have to change his "ways" if he wanted to live . . . he didn't and he died within a few years . . . I never got the chance to see him again after that night in Chicago, but he is often on my mind.

Florence was a wonderful person, and I particularly became very close to her during two summers of my high school years, when I worked with her and Paul at Glen Island beach. The beach was near the famous Glen Island Casino where Glen Miller and his orchestra, as well as other well-known "big bands," played in the late thirties. It was also near the "castle" where I would love to go with my family. It was such an enchanting place to visit, and I would love to scamper around the grounds trying to find a way in, which I never did. My father would tell us of the times when it was a German beer garden and how they would often go there on the weekends or in the evenings.

Grace lived next door to Aunt Louise and Florence with her husband, Danny (Pope), their two sons, Dominick (Porky) and Daniel (Dannyboy), and her mother-in-law. Although Grace was Irish, she was as much Italian as anyone in the neighborhood and she and Danny were two of the most caring and giving individuals in the West. I will never forget, however, the polenta and huge homemade ravioli her mother-in-law would make when we went there for dinner. Danny's brother, Mingo, lived on the second floor with his wife, Rita, and their three children, Ginger, John, and Sandra, who married Johnny DeMaz. I was his "best man" at the wedding, and godfather to their first child Debbie.

My mother spent a lot of time "discussing" matters with my Aunt Gertie and Grace. When she wanted Aunt Gertie, she would never call down the stairs for her; she would merely stomp down on a well-worn spot on the kitchen floor, and this was a signal for her to come upstairs. A conversation would follow and invariably they would soon be disagreeing on something or another. A discussion over the dispute could last for hours, days and even months, and eventually Grace would be dragged into the confrontation. The three of them would all be talking at once, and all you could hear was "Now Mary . . . ," "Now Gertie . . . ," "Now Grace . . ." None of them ever seemed to be listening to what the other(s) was saying.

Cooney was a "very robust" woman and had a stationery store on Fourth Street, next to Cancro's Funeral Home. Our older brother's spent a lot of time at Cooney's, as most of our time was devoted to Mickey's Stationery. Whenever we did go there, she would go out of her way to be nice to us. On some of these occasions, Mr. Cancro (who my father always said would "be the last man to let you down") would come in for his daily edition of the Standard Star, the hometown newspaper, and Billy Williams claimed that he would always go to the obituaries first . . . and smile.

Following is the only picture I could find of the club, and, unfortunately, it is not very clear. It was taken in my mother's kitchen, and include, from left to right, Florence, Feeney, Cooney, my mother, Lulu, Aunt Gertie, and Grace (who never stood still) in the foreground.

While I have referred to stories about various members of the family throughout the narrative, certain of the lineage deserve separate attention, such as "the aunts and uncles."

Chapter 9
The Aunts and Uncles

My father was born, I was always told, in the Little Italy section of New York City, but was raised in Tuckahoe, New York. My mother's family, the Codella's, settled in New Rochelle and they met while he was working on the trolley lines, which used to blanket the streets. He had four brothers and three sisters:

Louis—dubbed Noisey by Joe Calo, married to Aunt Gertie,

Thomas—Uncle Tuts or the Baron, married to Aunt Lilly Ramaglia,

James—married to Aunt Rose LaPorta,

John—married to Aunt Anna,

Caroline—Aunt Lena, married to Uncle Columbus (Bumbo) DeRosa,

Mary—Ma, married to Uncle Gennero (Gennarine) Poggiale, and

Michelina—married to Rocco Morsillo

Uncle Louie

As Aunt Gertie was my second mother, Uncle Louie was my second father. How clearly I can go back in my mind to the first floor apartment where they lived and walk through the kitchen to the living room, and see him sitting in a lounging chair watching television or, more likely, reading. He was so unlike my father, or the other uncles, as he had seen some of the world (from a porthole, as my father would always claim) during a stint in the navy. He had tattoos on his arms, and I particularly liked a sailing ship, which he would "sail" by flexing his muscles, such as they were . . . he was very thin, another distinguishing feature from my father. As the tale went, he had to gauge himself on bananas and milk to make the weight to get into the navy.

I would sit fascinated at his feet and listen to stories of his travels, while he showed me pictures of the far-away lands he had seen. Even then, I had a wanderlust which would stay with me all my life and which I would be lucky enough to fulfill (almost) as I was to see most of the ancient cities of Europe, the suks of Saudi Arabia, the beautiful panoramas of South America (particularly Rio de Janeiro), the golden sands of Hawaii and the Caribbean, the glaciers of Alaska and the overwhelming sights and smells of India.

He was an unrelenting "teaser" and nothing escaped his quick wit. I always felt he was very intelligent, although I believe he had little formal education. He was interested in a lot of things, especially sports, and was an excellent golfer, before he had to give it up. Most of his life was spent working at the A&P, and we (especially my father) waited for him to bring home "speckled" fruit each night. He also worked as a bartender at the Baron's.

Although he was very thin, he always had his pants button open, as he struggled for air due to his long bout with emphysema, which he was to lose in his early fifties. How I missed him.

Uncle Tuts

He became a part of family lore when he put the family cat into his "house," which happened to be the oven. Unfortunately, for the cat, my grandmother was not aware of this when she lit the oven to warm it in preparation for the evening meal. It was never made clear to me just how "well done" the poor pet was before someone realized (perhaps through a sense of smell—ugh!) where the missing cat was. I like to think it lived on to see better, but more likely worse, days.

Uncle Tuts always owned a bar and restaurant, as far as I know, and it was always called the Baron's. I vividly recall his place on River Street, and the warm feeling I would get in that old establishment (I told you I liked bars). I especially remember the free pretzels on the bar and a jukebox he had where, for a nickel; you not only got to hear your favorite song, but also were greeted by a moving picture image of a beautiful girl. He later moved to the Boston Post Road, in Larchmont, where he first had a place on the west side of the street, and later bought a building on the opposite side.

The Baron's was a very successful Italian restaurant, largely due to the fact that it was truly a family-run business. Uncle Tuts, Aunt Lillie (whose real name was Louise; however, she went by the name Lillian), and their two sons, Edward (Eddie) and Alphonse (Allie), were there all the time. Uncle Louie also worked there for a while as a bartender, and my nephew Steven as a waiter.

One of the non-family members who worked there for many years was a "pizza-man" by the name of "Dodo." I have no idea how he got that name—it didn't seem to have any relationship to his most obvious distinguishing feature—the flattest nose I have ever seen on a white man. Dodo spoke in a very gravely tone and when you asked him about the nose, he would say, "I got it looking through keyholes." Besides making great pizza and looking through keyholes, he had another talent: he could play the guitar and sing, and he was good enough to land a spot on a well-known television show of that era, The Arthur Godrey Talent Show. It was certainly exciting to actually see someone you knew on TV, and we all booed when Dodo lost the competition, after a moving rendition of his favorite song, "Felicia no compecia." I always felt he could have won if he had sung "One meatball." You don't know that one? It had the unforgettable line; "You get no bread with one meatball." I think Arthur Godrey would have loved that one; after all, his biggest hit was "Chalking Around," which explained how he made love to his overweight girlfriend by leaving chalk marks as he made his way around her large body, to keep track of where he had been. Did I say he had a classy show?

Another of his "pizza-men" in later years was "Big Al" . . . his distinguishing feature was the inside of his lips . . . where he had tattooed the name of one of his girlfriends. He became infatuated with my daughter Karen, who, together with my niece, Mary Ellen, hung out on Dillon Street, which was near the Baron's. The attraction for them was the fact that an abundance of good-looking teenage boys lived there. Big Al took it upon himself one night to drive up to our home in Stamford, Connecticut, park outside of the house, and to throw pebbles from my driveway at Karen's bedroom window. When I was awakened by Karen (never a good thing to do in the wee hours of the morning) to tell me what was going on out front, I put on my robe and stormed out of the front door. He immediately tried to take off down the street, but I stopped him before he could scurry away. It was soon obvious to me why he was called "Big Al," but this didn't stop me from reading him the "riot act." He was very civil to me, and I told him (with my fingers crossed behind my back) he was welcome in my home at any "reasonable" time of the day . . . I never saw him again . . . thank God.

My parents would often let us stay up late on Saturday nights and wait for Uncle Tuts and Aunt Lillie to arrive with pizza, after closing the restaurant. How I loved to see them (and not only because of the pizza), even though he, like many in my family, was a great "teaser" and especially took great glee in kidding me about my Dodgers (he was a Giant fan). Again, how lucky we were to be so immersed in our family and neighborhood.

Uncle Jimmy

Talk about characters? He definitely was one. He was short and stocky with a ruddy complexion and reddish hair, and lived in Mt. Vernon, where, among other things, he drove a cab and was a "Good Humor man." He had two children: James (Jackie) and Janet. We, unfortunately, never saw them very much; and after Uncle Jimmy retired, he and his wife, Rose, moved to Phoenix, Arizona, with Jackie and his family. I remember Jackie as having red hair and being very big (he was an all-county football star) and Janet as being small—with dark hair and complexion, like her mother—and beautiful.

Uncle Jimmy's stock-in-trade was his ability to make you like him instantly, primarily because he was such a "smooth-talker," or in the words of the street, a "bullshitter." He could really pour it on. He would suddenly show up in New Rochelle, generally at Aunt Lena's (she favored him and he knew it), and everyone in the family would swear they weren't going to have anything to do with him. However, he soon had them gushing over him as he complimented them on their looks, their clothes, and, with a definite ulterior motive, their cooking—he, like all Semenzas, "lived to eat."

Uncle Johnny

I, unfortunately, knew him least of all, as he was the antithesis of Uncle Jimmy, being soft-spoken and generally quiet and was clearly the "black sheep" of the family, having committed the ultimate atrocity: marrying an Irish woman. In those times, this was almost unheard of in the West, and my family never could quite accept it; they finally did. Aunt Anna was a truly wonderful, loving woman who bore five children, Winifred, Anna Loraine, Dudleen, John (Brother) and, my favorite, Richie.

My family did have one great fault: their intolerance of anyone who did not live the way they did. This even extended to my own life, as I broke the mold by bringing the first girl into 228 Union Avenue, being the first to marry, and, worst of all, moving from New Rochelle to Stamford, Connecticut. On her deathbed, my mother told me of a home in New Rochelle. She knew it would be perfect for my family; she died believing I would someday come to my senses and move back "home."

Uncle Johnny and his family lived in the "wilds" of Yonkers, New York. I will never forget their house and the warmth and memories it held for me. It seemed we only went there in the summer (I assume my father would never venture that far in the winter) and it was the closest I would ever come to "going to camp." There was so much to do there, from dangling on the swings which hung from the large trees in their yard, wandering off into the woods (where we would inevitably meet an old gentleman with a long beard, whom my father always said was a member of the "House of Lords"), feeding the chickens and pigs, exploring the hidden treasures in their cellar, including the first hunting rifle I had seen and held, and so on—these things did not exist in West New Rochelle.

I remember one particular occasion when I had enjoyed such a great time with my cousins that I convinced my mother and father to let me sleep over. It was great—we played monopoly and listened to the piano roll on the front porch, ate tomato and mayonnaise sandwiches, and had a wonderful time—until it was time to go to bed! Several of my cousins, their dog and me all piled into one huge feather bed. I just couldn't handle that and carried on so much that Aunt Anna had to call my father in the middle of the night to come and get me. The car trip from New Rochelle to Yonkers was comparable, for my father, to flying to Australia, and so you can imagine how that call was greeted. There was no doubt in my mind, however, that he would come to my rescue—and he did.

He and my mother were always there for all of us. In my early teens, I had gone out on a date with a girl who lived in the Bronx, and we went to the most spectacular movie theater I had ever seen: Lowe's Paradise. It was beautiful, and as you looked up at the ceiling, it was as if you were looking at the actual star-lit sky above you. This vividly came to mind as I read about the sky that opened above the great dining hall at Hogwarts in the magical Harry Potter novels. After leaving my date, I headed to catch the bus back to New Rochelle, as I was still too young to drive, and discovered to my utter dismay that I had missed the last one. It was too far to walk, and I had no choice but to call my father, who had probably fallen asleep several hours earlier while watching his favorite TV show, Alfred Hitchcock Presents. I, of course, had not told them where I was going that night, and all he kept saying over the phone was, "But what the deuce are you doing in the Bronx at one o'clock in the morning?" There was no doubt he would get dressed and drive all the way there to get me, albeit it would take forever—he did, and it did.

This wasn't the only time I got stranded after a "night out"—another memorable episode was after spending Friday night at the Mount Vernon roller skating rink. We loved to go there, and I can clearly remember the sound of the organ playing the latest hits of the day, including two of my favorites, the "Tennessee Waltz" and "Harbor Lights," and of the announcements made over the loudspeaker that the next skate would be for "Girls only," "Couples only," and so on. One evening, Kentucky (remember him?) and I met two girls at the rink, and went with them to the diner across the street and splurged on some dessert—they made the best cherry-cheese cake I have ever tasted (how do I remember that?) We then walked each of our "dates" home—my girl's name was Kitty Wool, whom I was never to see again—but how could I ever forget that name? When I met him back at the diner, we realized that each of us had "splurged" a little too much, and neither had any money left to take the bus back home—a very considerable distance. I just couldn't call my father—again. But it was much too far to walk, and so we decided to do the next best thing: skate home. We, of course, were true skating aficionados and carried our own skates in a colorful little case (I still have mine); however, they weren't made for the hazards of the city streets: they had wooden wheels. After several hours of dodging manhole covers, trolley tracks, dog shit, cars, and buses, we did arrive safely back in the West; my body still vibrates just writing about it.

Uncle Columbus (Bumbo)

Columbus, yes Columbus, DeRosa, my Aunt Lena's husband, was clearly one of the most unforgettable people I would ever meet. They had three children, Ralph (you'll hear a lot about him) Marie and Claudia. Aunt Lena's true name was Caroline, but, as with most members of my family, never went by that name (I actually was not aware that this was her name until a party given in her honor on her eightieth birthday.) Members of the DeRosa clan called her Aunt Betty, and I believe this was in reference to Uncle Bumbo's resemblance to Humphrey Bogart, who called his wife, Lauren Bacall, by her real name, Betty.

How would you characterize Uncle Bumbo? Colorful, animated, loquacious, extraverted, interesting, caring? All these and more. He would walk into a room and immediately become the center of attention—with a name like Columbus, how could he not be? Legend has it that his father lost a bet and had to pin that name on him. To his family, however, he was just Uncle Bumbo. Even now as I remember that name, I am filled with a rush of excitement thinking of how absorbed we would be by his enthusiasm and his outlandish antics and stories—he had a million of them, as they say, and could he relate them to his wide-eyed audience!

One of his great disappointments in life was that we did not have a lawyer in the family, or, as he would say, "We have enough accountants. What we need in the family is a legal crook."

A very special treat was to accompany him on his early morning milk route, where he was employed as a milkman for Sheffield Farms. There was something very exciting and yet peaceful about being with him in his truck—hearing the tingle of the glass bottles against the metal cases in the rear as he drove through the early morning fog; walking to the doorsteps of the silent houses; removing the used bottles and replacing them with clean cool new bottles of milk; and, best of all, listening to him tell, in uncharacteristic quiet tones, stories about his customers.

One of his favorite story themes was his unbelievable ability to expel wind (I'm being polite) with an explosive quality that wasn't matched until invention of the atomic bomb—it was awesome! One story I vividly remember him telling was an explosion he launched in an elevator when he thought he was out of range of any living targets, only to hear a poor unfortunate lady exclaim in an adjunct elevator, "Oh my god, what the hell was that?," as she gasped for a breath of fresh air. For his everyday "expulsions," he would routinely pin blame for the unpleasant odor on his faithful, always-by-his-side miniature bulldog terrier, Tippy.

Another of his antics was to remove his false teeth and chase us around the room with them; one of his favorite targets was my wife, Marie, who would run "like hell" with Uncle Bumbo and his teeth in hot pursuit.

It was always fun to go clamming or fishing with him in the wee hours of the morning (he, of course, was used to getting up early) in the waters of Long Island Sound. An invitation to go fishing with him, however, usually meant you had to first spend several hours untangling his lines from a prior excursion.

Uncle Bumbo was never known to turn down a drink. Although I never saw him, or any of my relatives, except for Uncle Gennarine, drink to excess, some of the old family pictures usually depicted him in a less-than-sober state, including the following photo, which is a classic.

It was taken on New Year's Eve in 1930, and the party was held in the home of Margaret Satallaro (according to the inscription on the back of the original). It includes many of those whom you have or will meet in this narrative, including:

Top row—left to right:
Charlie Mangano, Aunt Gertie, Gumma Francis, Feeney Mangano, Unknown, Netti Zari (Uncle Bumbo's sister), Next two—unknown, Aunt Lena, My father and mother

Next row:
Three people seated on the left—unknown
Little Anna Libertino and her husband, Canio; Lulu DeRosa is behind them, woman in front of my mother is unknown

Seated on the floor:
Uncle Louie, Unknown, Uncle Bumbo (passed out), Unknown, Paul Amato and Joe DeRosa (Lulu's husband)

Although he spent his younger life as a milkman, his later years were spent working for the City of New Rochelle in the supply room—that was somewhat like putting Dracula in charge of the blood bank! Ralph was, in many ways, very much his father's son and on many occasions even went Uncle Bumbo one further. For example, although I do not believe he ever took a tollbooth home from his job with the New York State Thruway, he did have the largest and strongest picnic table-top in the world—so what if across the top of it were the words:

> **EXIT 5**
> **LARCHMONT**
> **ONE MILE**

Uncle Bumbo's cellar looked like the home improvement department of Home Depot. This in fact inspired his son-in-law, Donald Vec (Vecchio), who was married to Marie, to launch a new career.

Donald Vecchio (Vec)

Vec's daytime job was also with the Thruway, and at one juncture, he was in charge of opening the bridge over the Hutchinson River Canal for the one or two barges that might pass by during the day and disturb his "artistic" pursuits. With all this spare time on his hands, he began to create miniature figures from the inexhaustible supply of available nuts and bolts, and other assorted junk, readily available in his father-in-law's cellar. He was truly a very unique and creative individual who, in his spare time, was also a driver for some local luminaries, including Peter and Mary Lind Hayes and their neighbors, Gordon and Sheila McCrae, who were Broadway and movie singing stars of the era. Peter was a well-known radio and TV personality who on occasion hosted a late-night television talk show. One night, as Vec was driving him to the TV studio in New York City, Peter noticed one of these creations lying on a car seat, and was impressed when Vec told him he had made it. He asked him to sit in the audience that evening, and during a lull in the show, Peter held up the nut-and-bolt figure and identified its creator as the new and budding artist . . . "El Vecchio." He then had Vec stand up and take a bow—how about that! As Vec would always say, "Peter must have been desperate for guests that night."

Vec would go on to make hundreds of these figures, which he would sell at craft shows for up to $100 each, and even made some for Peter's famous friends, including Frank Sinatra. He also received an offer to create a figure each month for a national promotion company, which he turned down as he felt this would stifle his creativity—I told you he was unique! Eventually he gave up making them, and went on to stained glass, as the "nut and bolt figure" market became flooded with imitators and, as he said "Unfortunately, you can't patent creativity."

Uncle Gennero Poggiale (Gennarine)

Uncle Gennarine was married to my father's sister Mary, whom we all called Ma. You had to love her; my eyes fill with tears just thinking about her now, although she has been gone for most of my life. She was such a gentle loving person and left us so early. She had four children—Alphonse (Fuzzy), Armand, Rose (Rosie) and Carmela (Looch). Gennarine was her complete opposite—he was, in my young eyes, a giant of a man whose great love in life was the opera, and more specifically an opera singer, the great Caruso. I remember listening to him on scratchy seventy-eight speed records, which Uncle Gennarine played incessantly. The real treat, however, was when he had had a few too many and would burst into an operatic aria in his booming baritone voice, as tears would stream down his large, flushed cheeks. He was to remarry after Ma's death; however, I have no recollection of his second wife.

The Brooklyn Connection

I never knew my father's third sister, Michelina, who lived in the Far Rockaway section of Brooklyn. I vividly remember, however, two of her three children, Columbia (Little Lena) and Alphonse (Fuzzy, referred to as the Fuzzy from Brooklyn so as not to confuse him with the other Fuzzy.) Her other child, Margaret (Gutt-ta-gutt) died at an early age, I believe.

I only have a vague recollection of visiting them in Brooklyn a few times, particular of going into a local pub, which had a beautiful mahogany bar, and nibbling on tasty pretzels and drinking a Coke from the dispenser. We would see Little Lena on occasions, as she was very close with Aunt Lena.

In order to assist the reader in identifying my family ties, the following is my humble attempt at a family tree:

Semenza Family Tree
Alphonse Semenza/Carmela Carpiento

Charles / Mary Codella
- Charles Jr.
- Robert

James / Rose LaPorta
- James Jr.
- Janet

Louis / Gertrude Codella
- Louis Jr.
- Ronald
- Carmela

John / Anna (?)
- John Jr.
- Winifred
- Anna Lorraine
- Dudleen
- Richard

Thomas / Louise (Lillian) Ramaglia
- Alphonse
- Edward

Caroline / Columbus DeRosa
- Marie
- Ralph
- Claudia

Mary / Gennero Poggiale
- Alphonse
- Armand
- Rose
- Carmela

Michelina / Rocco Morsillo
- Margaret
- Alphonse
- Columbia

And then there were—"the cousins."

Chapter 10
The Cousins

Ralph DeRosa

Ralph was undeniably . . . something else! He was my closest and favorite cousin while growing up (I am not including Ronnie and Louis who, as I have mentioned, were more like brothers). He was my age and very thin, a fact that will be hard to believe by those who only knew him in his adult years when he tipped the scales at three hundred plus pounds. Joe Calo pinned two nicknames on him: "Fatass" and "Ponzi." His son, Ralph Jr., wasn't far behind him in this regard and was always referred to, in relative terms, as "Little Ralph."

Ralph and I were in the same class at St. Joseph's until he "transferred" to Columbus School after the fifth grade. I am not sure what the real reason for this was, but it probably had something to do with his penchant for putting thumbtacks on the nun's chairs, or allegedly carving his initials on the back of the new church pews. I remember one episode when he put a tack under Sister Fabian's chair, our fifth grade teacher, but we were unfortunately not there to witness the outcome. The result was confirmed, however, when she stood red-faced in front of the class the next morning, and proclaimed, "Ralph DeRosa, step out into the hall." Ralph, with a feigned hurt look on his face followed her into the hall, and, as usual, denied having anything to do with the episode. He told her, however, that he did know who did it . . . and he pinned the blame on Dee Dee (Tedesco). Poor Dee Dee—he was very, very thin and was always getting picked on, and when his name was called out in class, he quickly tried to unsuccessfully defend himself by stating, in a very shaky voice, "But Sister, I put a yellow tack under your seat, and you sat on a red one." Mistake!

It was always an adventure to be with Ralph, especially on those very rare occasions when I got to sleep over at his house. They lived on the corner of Washington Avenue and Eight Street in what I remember to be a beautiful two-family white house. The Rispole family lived on the second floor. The focus of that family, however, as far as my story goes, was their son: Pissbones. He wore glasses and was even skinnier than Ralph, who took great pleasure in terrorizing him. Ralph had a great love of cars and was driving at the age of about twelve. The family car was kept in a garage behind their house and Ralph, one fine morning, invited me and Pissbones to "go for a ride." We were really impressed as he expertly opened the choke (this had to be done to the automobiles of that day, especially on cold mornings, to prime the carburetor) and started up the car with the keys he had "borrowed" from his father. He then put the car in gear, released the hand brake, and simultaneously raised his left foot up from the clutch while putting his right foot down on the accelerator. Whoosh! We bolted out of the garage and clear through the rear wall. He had put the car into reverse.

This minor setback didn't deter him from his love affair with automobiles and he was soon driving around the neighborhood eagerly willing to teach anyone how to drive. My cousin Louis took him up on this! Ralph carefully instructed Louis as to the rudiments of operating the vehicle and then told him to start the car and simply drive. Louis readily agreed and stepped on the gas. Whoosh! The car bolted out of the parking space, crossed over the traffic dividing line, ran onto the sidewalk and over the once-fine lawn of some unsuspecting elderly homeowners, coming to rest slightly within the confines of their living room. The one minor thing Ralph had neglected to mention to Louis was to straighten the wheels, so as to permit the car to move in a reasonably straight direction rather than in an uncontrolled u-turn.

Ralph also liked to demonstrate his driving mastery by seeing just how close he could come to someone without actually hitting them, like Officer (Cappy) Capellino! On one occasion, he was standing in the middle of the street directing traffic, as Ralph was "lurking" behind a line of cars waiting for him to "whistle-on" the traffic. When he did, Ralph proceeded to drive straight at him, only to veer past his spit-shined shoes at the very last moment—well, almost! I can still picture the surprised look on the officer's face as he stood there motionless, with his whistle clenched between his teeth, as he realized that one of the tires on Ralph's car had actually crossed over his foot. He came limping after us screaming, "If I didn't know your mother and father so well, I would toss you in jail and swallow the key."

Back to Pissbones. We would like to play cowboys and Indians with him. We were the cowboys, and he was the Indian! After one of our games, Ralph and

I were sitting contently in his living room, after a delicious dinner Aunt Lena had cooked, when Pissbone's mother appeared at the door, tearfully asking if we had seen Richie (that was his real name which, of course, only his mother and other grown-ups called him), as he had not come home for dinner. Ralph and I just stared at each other! Oh no! We had tied the Indian to the front of the car in retribution for his attack on our wagon train, but that was long before dinner, and he must have escaped since then—wrong. We told his mother not to worry and that we would go out to search for him. On taking the gag from his hungry mouth and releasing him, Ralph "convinced" him to conjure up an excuse for his tardiness, which he of course did.

The most memorable (and infamous) episode I ever shared with these two, however, was on the occasion of our Confirmation. This is the Sacrament of the Catholic Church that you receive after Baptism and Communion. Following is a photo of my mother and I on that latter day, with our home in the background.

Confirmation is a very serious affair, and it involves special religious instruction as to the significance of the Sacrament, choosing a middle name (I picked Anthony after my favorite Saint) and selecting a sponsor who accompanies you during the ceremony. I selected my cousin Allie. All of my cousins were very special to me and he was no exception. Unfortunately, Allie, who always seemed to be such a happy-go-lucky guy, was to desert his wife, Dolly, and children and just disappear. I was never to see him again, although he did call me years later asking for money. He surely broke the hearts of his family and was never truly forgiven, even after his death at a relatively early age. Dolly, who was always very thin and never looked healthy, also died prematurely. Following is a photo of Allie and me on my Confirmation day.

Confirmation was also an excuse to hold an elaborate party in honor of the recipients of this beautiful Sacrament, and my mother and father busily made all the necessary arrangements for the celebration, which was to take place at our house. On the morning of the Confirmation, we had to go to Mass and receive Holy Communion to prepare for the Sacrament. I was there bright and early to make certain I would get a seat close to the altar to make sure I didn't miss anything. Unfortunately, Ralph, who was on crutches at the time, as he had broken his leg, and Pissbones spotted me up front and decided to join me. What a mistake!

The Mass dragged on as usual and we all started to get a little restless, as we wanted the ceremony to hurry along so we could get to the main event, which was scheduled for later in the day. What happened next has always been a matter of great controversy in our family, namely, who started pinching who? There has never been any doubt in my mind that it was Ralph. It certainly wasn't Pissbones, and just consider Ralph's reputation! In any event, someone started it and soon we were pushing and shoving each other, but without making it obvious to anyone around us. We thought we were safe—wrong.

Who would have guessed that Father Botti, who was so absorbed in the celebration of the Mass, would have ever taken notice of the "goings-on" in the front pew! Legend has it that during the most important part of the Mass, the Consecration, as he was solemnly lifting the chalice over his head, he spied our images in the shiny goblet. I do, however, vividly remember what he did next, regardless of how anyone thought he saw us. He whirled around (the altar didn't face the multitude at that time) and in a very loud voice proclaimed, "Youa boys, get outa the churcha [he also spoke in broken English]!" Wow, this was exciting! This had never happened in the entire history of our world. We whirled around to see who the unlucky culprits were, secretly enjoying the misery they would soon endure. Father Botti shouted again, a little more specifically, "Youa three aboys, get outa the churcha." No one moved. Father Botti then started pointing in our general direction, as we continued to innocently look around the church for the unfortunate trio. His face, which was normally very red, got redder and redder until, at last, he called over one of the altar boys, Bobeep (Cassone). Although he was very large, Bobeep looked like a mountain as he walked off the altar and straight at us—oh my god, I thought! He grabbed each of us by the back of our necks (I told you he was large) and escorted us straight up the center aisle and past the standing-room only crowd of worshipers. The only consolation for me was that my mother was not at the Mass, as she was home probably making meatballs for the party to be given in my honor, but I did spot my Cousin Rosie as she swooned into someone's arms when she recognized who was being led up the aisle.

Can you imagine how I felt as I reached the top of the stairs in front of the church? My world had ended (at least that's what I was thinking). What a disgrace! There was just no way I could ever go home again and I just wandered away from the general direction of the church trying to decide what I should do. I have no idea just how long I walked around until I finally decided that I had to go home to "face the music." As usual, there were a lot of people at my house as I sheepishly walked up the stairs and into the kitchen, fully expecting the worse; it wasn't that bad. After my mother uttered a few words, which I never heard her say before or after, she tearfully threw her arms around me and hugged me. She had been truly worried about me, and, anyway, as she said . . . "it must have been Ralph's fault!"

All's well that ends well, and I did make my Confirmation, with my two "buddies," after we officially apologized to Father Botti. During the ceremony, the priest ceremoniously and gently slaps your cheek, but I distinctly recall getting an extra hard slap that day.

There was another infamous "episode" involving an aunt of Pissbones who lived on St. John's Place. She had both a dog and a canary, and would entertain guests by having the dog "kiss" the tiny yellow bird while she held it in her hand. I guess the dog got tired of playing second fiddle to a bird, and one day when it was being prompted to smooch up to the canary, he went one step further; he bit its head off, leaving the shocked aunt with the remaining parts of the departed bird's small body in her still outstretched hand.

Ralph also had an affinity for fires, especially ones that could be started in my mother's kitchen. Although my recollection of the actual event is somewhat clouded, I do remember Ralph conning my grandfather into giving him some of those wooden matches which Italian men used to light up their "guinea stinkers." Although I have tried, I have never been able to light up a match the way he could, by striking it against his rump. We were able to light one by more conventional means, however, and while the grownups were downstairs, we decided to start a little campfire on the kitchen floor. Fortunately for all concerned, someone either smelled smoke or came up to check on us and the fire was put out after causing only minor damage to the linoleum.

He and I were also altar boys. Fortunately for the church, there were only a few times when we had the opportunity to serve Mass or other ceremonies together. I do remember one occasion when we were together at an evening novena and Father Botti (him again?) kept motioning for us to back away from him. We kept creeping backward on our knees, but he continued to "shoo" us farther and farther away until we were almost off the altar. Apparently, he was under the mistaken impression that the more distance there was between him and us, the least likely it was that we would get into some sort of mischief (some priests never learn). Ralph and I were doing our best to pay attention to the Latin, but he kept complaining about how hot it was in the church. I didn't feel very warm but he kept "bitching" about it until I happened to glance back into the church and suddenly understood the reason for his discomfort: he was on fire! Father Botti had backed him right into a rack of candles. All hell (I guess it would be heaven in church) broke loose as it seemed the entire congregation noticed the "extra candle" on the altar at the same time. Someone had the presence of mind to roll him up into a rug that was on the altar and was able to quench the flames with Ralph experiencing only minor injuries, most of which were to his pride.

His appetite was unbelievable. As Uncle Bumbo once said to him, "If you could cook shit, you'd eat it." After one late night eating binge in the Thruway Diner on Main Street, where he downed a dozen eggs, he announced that he wanted to go to the bathroom but not to just any bathroom. It had to be the one at Tuffeneti's, a famous Italian restaurant in Times Square . . . that's right, the one in New York City. He said it was beautiful, and best of all it had some type of blue light which shown on the toilet seat to keep it sanitized. Believe it or not, we drove all the way to the City and back so that he could have a pleasant bowel movement . . . he could not have had "to go" very bad!

His size came in very handy at times, especially on one occasion when we were running from the angry shouts of a "neighbor" who didn't appreciate our "visit" to his "orchard" to taste the delicious apples. We didn't have to climb his fence in order to escape. Ralph didn't slow down one iota as he smashed into the fence, dragging it along as we laughingly ran through the fields to freedom.

Although Ralph and I were to remain very close friends into our early twenties, and he was to be the "best man" at my wedding, and I at his, and he godfather to my first-born, and I to his, we drifted apart, especially when I moved to Stamford, Connecticut. In fact, for a real or imagined reason I was never to fully understand, his attitude toward me grew very antagonistic. Although I always claimed this didn't bother me, it did. I tried several times to get to the root of his feelings—calling him on Christmas and getting him aside at wakes—all to no avail. Ralph contracted Hodgkin's disease and suffered greatly during most of his adult years. When he was hospitalized for what I knew would be the last time, I had to give it one more try. Marie and I visited him in New Rochelle Hospital, and we reminisced about the old times. As we were leaving, I reached out to touch his hand, and he looked at me and said, "Chesty, you've come a long way." Perhaps . . . perhaps I had my answer.

Louis Semenza

You have already heard a lot about Louis, but I could probably write a book just about him. He was truly one of the most outstanding athletes to ever come out of the West. He was a three-letter man at Isaac E. Young High School—basketball, baseball and football—and excelled in every sport he attempted, from golf to high-board diving. He was best, however, at basketball, and back in the pre-jump shot era, had one of the best "two-handed set shots" in the county. He was surrounded by a wealth of talent at Isaac, and there was nothing more exciting than watching the team play to a packed, screaming crowd at the New Rochelle Armory. Uncle Louie, Ronnie, and I would arrive there early to get a good seat, and patiently sit through the Junior Varsity game, until the moment when the band would strike up the school theme and the cheerleaders and Louis, the captain, would lead the team onto the floor in their beautiful green and white satin uniforms. Watching Louis play, however, was an adventure, as you never knew if he would be around by the end of the game. If my nemesis in life was a caddy master, his was a coach, namely Lou Amonson. It was never any great surprise to us when Louis failed to return to the court after half time following an argument with the coach.

After a game, if you asked Louis how many points he had scored, he would reply, "How do I know . . . do you think I have time during the game to keep track of my points?" He would then scour the Standard Star the next day to find the box score for the game, and heaven help us if it was wrong, as he would scream, "I had twenty-one points; they left out that foul shot I made at the end of the first quarter!" So much for not keeping track.

If I had to identify just two other things about Louis that stood out the most, I would have to select his appetite and his grandiose ideas. What an appetite! He would, for example, warm up for Thanksgiving dinner by downing several hot dogs at Walter's famous hot dog stand (it is still there)in nearby Mamaroneck. His most legendary eating accomplishment, however, took place at Trader Vic's in New York City, where he and Bobeep (remember him) gulped down an enormous multicourse meal, and when the waiter inquired as to how they enjoyed it, he replied "It was great . . . do it again."

My father would especially be amused by Louis's enthusiastic "ways," and his penchant for overexaggeration. He would laugh as he would tell tales of Louis . . . running into the house tearfully complaining that Junior had "hit me with a brick," which he would describe by holding his hands out as far apart as they could go and then bringing them back to within a miniscule inches of each other, or running into the house and breathlessly proclaiming, "Uncle Charlie, Uncle Charlie, the birds are singing; spring is here."

Although he had an athletic scholarship to college, he never did finish, as he was just too impatient to sit through four years of study . . . he had too many other ideas he wanted to explore. He would stampede into the house and begin to explain, with unbridled optimism, his latest scheme . . . from a fast food hamburger stand (MacDonald's beat him to it) to equipping envelopes with a little string to make them easier to open (I think someone actually did that). When I said he "stampeded" into the house, I mean that literally. He would never just open the front door and stroll through the hallway to the door to the ground floor apartment . . . he would charge in so fast that both doors could be heard simultaneously slamming shut! I could never figure out whether he just couldn't wait to eat something or to explain his latest idea(s), or whether, more likely, he was just afraid of someone or something lurking in the hallway to spring out at him.

He drifted through several jobs, including an elevator operator at Yonkers Raceway, where he complained, "I hate those guys who get into the elevator and just point their thumbs up without saying a word. What do they think I am, an elevator operator?" He just saw himself as something else.

After a stint in the Post Office, he made a major career decision to leave the security of a government position for a job in New York City (closer to Trader Vic's) in the field of color photography. I was very proud of his courage to make that change, and although I believe he did very well in this field, it was hard to tell from talking with him. He was always changing firms, going back to ones he had left, and complaining about his superiors. I would occasionally run into him in the City, generally in front of a hot dog stand. He never stopped dreaming, however, especially of living in Westport, Connecticut, where one of his many bosses resided.

Louis and his wife Josephine (Jo), who was one of the many who would come to our house to pay the insurance premiums to my father, had four children, Louis, Susan, Anthony and Paul.

Richie Semenza

Richie, the youngest son of my Uncle Johnny, stayed at our house for a few days one summer (and slept in bed alone) and a shining moment of his stay will live with me for as long as I live (as I know it stayed with him until his premature death from diabetes). As I have mentioned, the Boys Club had a summer baseball league, and you already know of my exploits as a player—but I was a great manager! We had a terrific team, led by my cousin Ronnie, and during Richie's visit, we had a game scheduled with our closest rival, and we were one player short. Richie had brought his "glove" along and readily agreed to play, assuring us of his prowess in the field and at the bat. We led throughout the game and went into the final inning with a thin lead. Our pitcher, however, got into trouble in that inning, and their best hitter, Johnny Lee, came to bat with several runners on base. Richie was playing centerfield and Johnny hit a tremendous shot in his general direction. Richie seemed to be thoroughly confused and simply ran around in circles, as the ball climbed higher and higher and kept going farther and farther away from him. It was hopeless—the game would be lost—and so we thought. But first let me tell you a little more about that "glove." It was not only ancient and devoid of any semblance of padding, but was barely larger than his left hand—he might as well have been playing barehanded. In any event, he continued to circle the now descending ball in whose general vicinity he had somehow managed to arrive. I never believed he actually saw the ball, but just as it was about to land on his head, he stuck out that glove, either in self-defense or to shield his face from the sun, and unbelievably the ball landed right into the pocket of his now-famous mitt. We—and, most of all, Johnny Lee, who was well on his way around the bases—were stunned; and, for a moment, no one moved. Then all hell broke loose as we rushed out to pound our hero on the back and carry him off the field. In his never-to-be-forgotten words, he breathlessly shouted, "I had it all the way." We never did get to see him play again—that would have only spoiled it.

Joe Calo

How blessed we were to have Looch, the youngest of my aunt Ma's children, marry Joe Calo. How can I possibly describe him? He was tall (next to the Semenza's) and handsome, and was always dressed with a shirt and tie. He was a great golfer, had a magnetic personality and you liked him as soon as he spoke, and he was seldom quiet. He was famous for giving everyone a nickname (his nickname was "chickencorn") and for his "ways". He was always carrying on about something or another, whether it was the problems with his job at Fort Slocum (now called Davids Island), and later at Fort Totten; his never-quite-to-be-fulfilled promises to have us play golf at Bonnie Briar golf course, where he was an Assistant caddie master to Sal and Joe DiBuono; his way of mimicking people, especially those few he didn't like, principally,

Sal and Joe DiBuono; his unfailing habit of buying only a dollar's worth of gas for his car just as he was about to run dry; his annual late evening arrival at my brother's home on April 15 to have his tax return done—well, you get the picture?

He was such a part of our family that it is hard not to think of him as anything but a Semenza! He truly loved my mother and father and mourned their passing, in some respects, more than anyone else in the family. He could not speak about them without getting tears in his eyes. He lived into his eighties, but died within his heart many years before when he lost his Looch.

I will never forget the day he died. I was taking a shower and suddenly thought about something he told me when I was very young—he claimed he had never lost his hair as he would always let the shower water hit the back of his head, rather than the top of his head (I warned you about his ways). As I was thinking about this, while the water was hitting the top of my head, I had a strong feeling that he had died. At that precise moment, the phone rang—it was Charlie. A call from him bearing news of someone's demise was not rare; however, I startled him when I mentioned my premonition about Joe—he was silent for a few moments and I knew—Chickencorn had left us.

Armand Poggiale

Opposite is a picture of Joe Calo (on the right), and my cousin, Armand Poggiale, the brother of Looch and Rosie, in their uniforms. We were so proud of our loved ones who were serving in the war, and of the "stars" which the families would display in their windows for each of them. I was, of course, partial to the navy and would gush with pride and admiration when Armand would come home on a furlough and tell us stories about his adventures at sea, including one about how the destroyer he was stationed on, the Blakely, was torpedoed. Only the front part of the ship was destroyed, however, and they were able to make it safely back to port. Unfortunately, according to Armand, all the gifts he was bringing home to the family were in that part of the ship.

I never saw much of Armand, as when he married, he and his wife, Eleanor (Durkin—an American) moved to New Jersey, and changed their name from Poggiale to Palmer (you can imagine how that went over in my family), and had a daughter, Gertrude (a.k.a. Elaine). Although I didn't see him as much as I would have liked to, I always looked up to him and totally enjoyed his visits, even though he never did bring me home a gift.

Johnny DiPippo

Johnny was married to Looch's sister, Rosie and was, of course, Joe Calo's brother-in-law. No two people could have been more dissimilar. Johnny was as serious as Joe was light hearted. The one thing they shared most in common was Fort Slocum. Joe worked there for most of his career, and during World War II, Johnny landed what had to be the most enviable job in the service—captain of the ferryboat, which ran from the mainland to the island where the fort was located. Imagine spending the entire war on a ferryboat and only fifteen minutes from your home. Besides marrying Rosie, however, this was probably one of the few good things to ever happen to Johnny during his lifetime.

Fort Slocum is deeply engrained in our family tradition, going back to the First World War, when my father was stationed there. As the story goes, he left the base one night to go on a date with my mother; however, he didn't have a pass. For this infraction, he was thrown into the "brig," and while he was serving his time, his unit shipped out . . . to join the troops fighting the war in Europe.

We were fortunate to be spared many of the tragedies that befall families, but the ones we had all seemed to fall on the shoulders of Johnny and Rosie. He suffered from depression and also had some financial difficulties, at least for a while. When Marie and I returned from our Florida honeymoon, and still had some money left over from the "aboost" we had received at our wedding, we loaned some of it to them as we knew they were going through a tough time. I know they never forgot this gesture. Marie and I always cherished their love for us.

Johnny died of a heart attack, in the arms of my brother and I at my home in Stamford, Connecticut, during a graduation celebration for my daughter, Barbara. I will always cherish the note she sent to us on his death—it read:

> Dear Marie & Bobbie
> From your home Johnny was called to his heavenly home. His final hours were spent in joy with the ones he loved. In God's care now, he realizes that our Lord loved him even more than we did. He prays for all of us now until once again we are united in joy, forever.
> Always,
> Rosie

Her heartaches were just beginning as she was left with the care of her three small grand children on the premature deaths of her son, Johnnyboy, and his wife. Her daughter, Carolyn, was also to have a difficult and lonely life, after her first marriage ended in divorce and she lost custody of her two children.

Marie was very close with Looch and Rosie, and always had difficulty talking about them without her eyes filling with tears.

Alphonse Poggiale (Fuzzy)

Fuzzy, the other brother of Looch and Rosie, was married to Ann (Salvati), and they had three children, Paul, Leonard and Marlene, all of whom went to college.

He was a Fuller brush man, a profession he was well suited for as he had the "gift of gab." He had a lot of interests and was never at a loss for words. When I was growing up, they lived only a block away, down at the bottom of the Second Street hill. I would love to go to their house, especially to look through his collection of sports cards and magazines, and to sit wide-eyed, as he told me stories about athletes I could only read about in Sport, the favorite magazine of the era (Sports Illustrated wasn't around yet.) He actually saw Babe Ruth hit home runs and was there the day Lou Gerhig, dying of a disease that was to be named after him, uttered his famous farewell words, which echoed through the stands of a packed Yankee Stadium, "Today, I consider myself the luckiest man on the face of the earth." Incidentally, Lou Gerhig lived in the south side of New Rochelle, and Marie and I rented rooms in an apartment house where he was said to have once lived, and where a street is named in his honor.

Best of all, Fuzzy would take me to the Polo Grounds to see the hated Giants play my beloved Bums and other National League teams. I vividly remember one particular game that went into several extra innings, before the Giants beat the Pittsburgh Pirates on a steal of home plate. What made that game so memorable for me was the starting pitcher and third basemen for Pittsburgh, Preacher Roe and Billy Cox, who were later traded to the Dodgers where they had outstanding careers.

The Car

Any tale about my family would be incomplete without mention of "the car" . . . my father's pride and joy . . . a 1937 (or thereabouts) Chevrolet. He had it for over twenty years and I guess would have kept it for another twenty if Charlie and I hadn't finally convinced him to trade it in for a sparkling new green Plymouth. That Chevy was something else, with standard shift, running boards and a small window on the driver's side, which could be cranked open to let in some air without opening the larger window. Although these windows were common in the cars of that era, his was not . . . it was filled with beautiful streaks of bright hues, much like a stained glass window . . . we never knew how this had happened. What it didn't have were a heater, a radio or, of course, air conditioning.

There was no mistaking Charlie Semenza's car on those rare occasions when he actually drove it, and at speeds never exceeding roughly twenty-five miles per hour. The car spent a lot of time parked in front of our house as my mother would try to talk my father into driving her someplace . . . generally to Main Street to go shopping. The mere hint of asking him to drive about five miles to Main Street would bring on a typical reaction, as he would rant and rave, "Main

Street? . . . Main Street? . . . Why I'd sooner drive you to Valhalla!" I told you he hated crowds. He also had a unique way of driving in the wintertime . . . it was called "wait for spring."

His "snail-speed" driving was legendary. When I was finally allowed to drive, I was totally amazed at how so many of the places he drove us to were actually very close to home—it always took forever to get anywhere when he was behind the wheel. When I moved to Stamford, Connecticut, he would have to drive up on U. S. Route 1, as he had been banned from the Merritt Parkway (he would never even consider using the New England Thruway) for obstructing traffic by driving too slow.

The new Plymouth? I was initially too young to drive the new car and it became the apple of Charlie's eye . . . it was truly a thing of beauty, until two things, totally beyond his control, happened . . . the Korean War and, even worse, my learning to drive. In those days this was truly a challenge, as you had to learn how to master the standard shift, which was not an easy task, especially when you had to let out the clutch on a steep hill. My father had a unique way of teaching, however, as he would subject us to about a year of "dry runs" on a kitchen chair to perfect our timing, before he actually allowed us to get behind the wheel of a real car. Anyway, I persevered and finally learned to drive while Charlie was off defending the world against Communism, after serving his basic training at the Sampson Air Force Base in upstate New York (where Louis also served). His last words to us as he left for the service were "Take care of the Plymouth." Sure!

In every letter we received from him, he would always end it by inquiring about the car, from which he had been so unfairly separated. My mother always assured him that the car was fine (I wonder if she ever confessed that "white lie"). It had, however, fallen into the clutches of someone who viewed the car for what it was—something to simply get you from here to there, namely, me.

Its demise started the day my father finally allowed me to take the car out at night . . . alone. After reminding me innumerable times to be careful, to which I readily agreed innumerable times, I drove off to pick up my friends and headed straight to a traveling carnival in the south end of town. After having a great time on the rides, playing the games and watching the sideshows, we headed back to the car which was parked in an open field. Unfortunately, the ground had gotten very soft from a heavy rain, and I was having trouble getting the rear wheels out of the mud. I decided that the best way to get out would be to go backward, and I put the car in reverse and stepped on the gas. Whoosh! It worked—almost. I shot out of the rut but the car was brought to an abrupt halt—I had hit something. What is the most unlikely object anyone taking his father's car (which was also the love of a brother who was off fighting a war in a foreign country) out for the first time could possibly hit . . . a trailer filled with carnival clowns, more specifically . . . midget clowns! I have always been somewhat apprehensive about clowns, especially midgets, but I was not prepared for what happened next, as they steamed out of their tilted trailer and began banging on the body of the car with their small hands and, unfortunately, with their even smaller hammers. God, were we scared as I put the car into low gear and sped off into the darkness dragging several of these furious Munchkins with me. I was certain I had left a few of them for dead and that the Standard Star would carry a headline the following morning, which would read "Midget Massacre at the Midway." Fortunately, it didn't, but I don't believe my father ever quite believed my cover story about the unbelievable violent, albeit local, hailstorm that caused all those small dents in the car. He just stood in front of the car shaking his head and murmuring, "What are we going to tell Junior?" We never had the heart to tell him, while he was in Korea, and I even sent him carefully edited photos of the more presentable portions of the car.

When Charlie returned home and looked at the car, he wanted to cry, but fortunately his love for me must have overshadowed his love for the car and he forgave me . . . I think. In any event, he had all that money he had saved during his four years in the Air Force, together with the money he had been saving since Baptism, and he bought the true love of his life (before Terry), a gorgeous turquoise and white Olds "eighty-eight" . . . funny . . . I never got to drive it.

Here is a picture of me and the good side of the car, which was taken in the driveway at Marie's family home on seventeen St. Joseph's Street.

Following are some of those old faded pictures of family and friends from the 1940s:

These pictures were taken at a picnic in the "wilds of Yonkers" where my Uncle Johnny lived.

Reading from left to right and from top to bottom:

1. Standing—Aunt Anna (Uncle Johnny's wife), Aunt Mary (Ma), Grace Grosso (told you she was a good friend), and Charlie
   Sitting—Dudleen and Richie (two of Uncle Johnny's five children), and Ronnie

2. Aunt Gertie, Uncle Louie, Ronnie, and Louis

1. Ronnie (in the front); Frankie Williams and me (second row); Charlie and Louis (third row), and Georgie Williams (in the back)

2. Allie (Uncle Tuts's son), Marie* and Charlie
   Me, Ralph*, and Ronnie

   * Uncle Bumbo's children

What must be quite obvious by now, is the fact that we all enjoyed an even much larger family—the family of the West. You have already met a lot of the characters who filled those carefree streets and heard many of the stories which enriched my childhood—however, there are some which merit special consideration and have earned, in my mind, a place in "Legends of the West."

Chapter 11
Legends of the West

There were so many memories of my formative years in the West, which I have tried to capture in these pages. There are some that were so special, however, that they deserved their own chapter, namely, the "whatever-you-need man," the home remedies, the neighborhood pranks, the habits and best of all, some final words on the "characters."

The "Whatever You Need" Man

Before the invention of refrigerators, every household had an "icebox," which, in our house, was tucked away in a little alcove off the kitchen. An "iceman" would make his neighborhood rounds in a truck, and supply the ice. His visits were eagerly awaited by all the neighborhood kids, especially during the hot, humid days of summer. We would suck on the ice chips which flew into the air as he expertly used his trusty pick to cut off sections of the large ice blocks, which he would get from the "icehouse" (that was a fun place to visit). He would carefully lift a block with his tongs, wrap it in a burlap cloth, carry it into the house, and put it in the icebox. Whatever the cost of an ice block was (ten cents I believe), it was worth it, considering the fascination his visits provided.

This was an age before the proliferation of shopping malls, super and discount stores, and the Internet—when various "men" would personally deliver most of the necessities of life directly to the doorstep. They truly provided an unparalleled personal service, as they would arrive at all hours of the day and enter the inner confines and confidence of our home and would, necessarily, become an integral part of everyday life. It wasn't simply a product or a service they provided—they were also a live, instant news-service as to the latest happenings in the neighborhood. They had the up-to-the-minute information on all the important happenings, such as who was born or had died, who had a new TV or radio, etc. In fact, most of their time was spent "discussing" these events rather than in selling their wares.

But who were these men? They included the following (sorry, feminists . . . they were all men):

Milkman
Laundry man
Coal man
Bread man
Egg man
Crystalline man
Knife sharpening man
Diaper man
Radio repair man
Iceman
Ragman
Fuller brush man—my cousin Fuzzy was one
Insurance man—my father was one
Bungalow Bar man—for some reason, the Good Humor man never came to the West, but a funny little truck with a "house" on the top of the roof did, and we would wait in line for a "Bungalow bar"—if we got a "lucky stick" we were entitled to a free ice cream bar, and my favorite . . . Dave "the Jew"

His Saturday morning visits were especially awaited. He was very tall, had a neatly trimmed mustache and was always meticulously dressed in the latest fashions. He had to be as he operated a clothing store on Main Street, "Famous Outfitters." My mother and aunt, and the whole neighborhood, belonged to his "club," and would pay him a small amount each week, which he would enter on a small card. This was a combination "installment plan," "savings plan," "lay-a-way plan," and "credit-card system" all in one.

Best of all, you got to talk to Dave. He would usually have a few samples with him—jockey shorts, ties, socks, and shirts. However, we would have to go to his store to make major purchases, such as our church and school pants, and that was just not as much fun. He seemed different when he was in a real business establishment.

And then there was the" Goat man." He, of course, did not come into the house but was a special sight to behold. He kept a small flock of goats in a fenced-in area on Union Avenue, between Fifth and Sixth Streets. I never knew why, but I assumed he used the goat milk and cheese for his own consumption, as I never knew anyone who bought these from him. He would proudly parade his goats straight down Union Avenue, take a right turn down Second Street hill and arrive at his "grazing grounds," an open field across from the plywood factory and just beyond the railroad overpass. These "goat drives" were unmistakable, even if you were unfortunate enough not to have witnessed them first-hand. The route was undeniably marked by a trail small round soft black pellets which the goats expelled as they merrily strolled to their noonday repast (presumably to make more pellets).

Home Remedies

As I said earlier, there wasn't too much we couldn't get within a few yards of our front steps, including miraculous cures. For every day "run-of-the-mill" illnesses, such as colds, flus, etc., we would simply call in Dr. Wartels (an American). He was straight out of a Norman Rockwell painting and one of the last of the true family physicians. He was available at any time of the day or night and all for $4 a visit. There was nothing more comforting than to be lying in your bed with a fever and to hear his cheery voice outside of your bedroom door. There was no mistake as to who it was. He was always in a hurry and would invariably knock something over or mistakenly walk into a closet, but he would always cure us, more by his reassuring manner, I believe, than from his medical prowess.

But for a real illness, like the "worms" or "getting overlooked," MDs were useless and you had to call in a neighborhood specialist and/or rely on home remedies. A typical scenario might begin when I would wake up in the morning, preferably on a school day, either with a queasy feeling in my stomach and not feeling very hungry (that was always enough to quickly convince my mother that I wasn't right), or with a slight fever (referred to by my father as a "cat fever"). My parents would begin to ask a lot of questions about my general state-of-being before putting me to the ultimate test, the delivery of a feces stool for their detail examination. They would then discuss my situation with Aunt Gertie, or whoever else might be in the kitchen having coffee, and then sadly announce the diagnosis.

Worms?

In all my adult years, I have never encountered another case of the worms or even found anyone who had even vaguely heard of them. Were they limited to West New Rochelle? Once the diagnosis was confirmed, however, there was only one remedy—a visit to the "worm-man." He actually didn't live in the neighborhood and I had to be driven to his house on River Street in the eastern section of the city. This street was somewhat of an extension of the West, however, as my Uncle Tuts had a bar and restaurant there at one time, and my cousin's (Johnny DiPippo) family lived there. I would be led into the house where everyone spoke in whispered tones—after all, this was serious! The "worm-man" seemed ancient to me, and would lead me to a small table, have me remove my shirt and expertly begin to probe my belly (mine took a lot of probing), and then place his ear against my stomach (in order to hear the worms, I guess). He would then knowingly shake his head in an affirmative way (I had them) and begin the cure. He would place a little olive oil on my amble belly and mutter a few words in Italian. When he was finished, he would discuss my condition with my parents and, more importantly, receive his fee, usually a bottle of homemade "guinea-red" wine. We had no need for managed health care. Actually, I recall very few personal bouts with the worms; however, Charlie seemed to get them a lot.

Overlooked?

They could also conclude that I might be "overlooked," especially if I complained of having a headache. The genesis of this illness was quite clear—someone had "overlooked" me, namely said or thought something complimentary about me. I, of course, wasn't aware of this at the time or I would have warded off the compliment by giving the unthinking individual the "horns," that is, pointed the index and pinkie fingers of either hand at them. The "horns" could also be store-bought and worn around your neck as a guaranteed, "24/7" safeguard against being "overlooked."

Once I was suspected of having been "overlooked," there was only one way to confirm and cure it—a visit to someone with "the power"—the "Mal Occhio Lady." Before my mother was able to obtain "the power," which could only be conveyed by a bona fide, "Mal Occhio Lady" on New Year's Eve, we had to go across the street to Mrs. Williams or, as she was more commonly referred to, Billy Williams's mother. Everyone's parents were identified in this manner, and I can't remember ever hearing the first name of any parent in the neighborhood.

I don't believe this was out of any disrespect, but rather from a view we had of considering parents as just an extension of each kid in the neighborhood. Their existence, in our young minds, was only due to the fact that they were the mother or father of a particular friend.

The "Mal Occhio Lady" would have me sit at a small table and make the sign of the cross on my forehead with her thumb, while murmuring some prayers in Italian. She would then place a few drops of olive oil into a small bowl of water and carefully study the circles that formed on the surface. She would then invariably announce that I was indeed "overlooked." If you were too ill to be taken across the street to Mrs. Williams, the diagnosis and ultimate cure could also be arranged by sending over an article of your clothing, as long as you had worn it while you had the symptoms.

Although we would always chide our mother for practicing "witchcraft," the cure was undeniable. This may in reality have been a true test of the power of persuasion, as you always felt a lot better as soon as you were even touched by the "Mal Occhio Lady," and you made a rapid recovery soon thereafter.

For many of our other illnesses where Dr. Wartels or the other neighborhood specialists were not needed, our mother would take care of the cure herself with various home remedies. In many cases the cure was a lot worse than the actual illness, and, because of this, I was very reluctant to feign too many of them to try to get out of going to school . . . that was a much safer place to be. For example:

Stomachaches

The obvious cure for this was an enema—reinforcements had to be called in to give one to me as I would rant and rave at even the slightest hint that they were thinking about it. Aunt Gertie was usually enlisted, and the only way I would ultimately submit to this drastic procedure was if they promised to buy me something. I vividly remember holding out on one occasion for an Indian outfit and a bow-and-arrow set—it wasn't worth it! For those lucky few in the world who have never had the experience, and I promise not to go into the lurid details, it basically involves filling your stomach with warm water injected by a tube placed into the bodily opening diametrically opposite your mouth. When your stomach is at the bursting point . . . forget about it.

Sore Throats

An equally unfortunate fate could greet me if I announced that I had a sore throat. Another instrument of torture was kept in the house to cure this—"a throat-swabber." This was a nasty looking little wire gadget, around which my mother would wrap cotton and dip it into some awful-tasting substance called augural. While someone held me down, as again I was usually not a willing patient, the brush was forced into my mouth and my throat was "swabbed," as I helplessly gagged. If my throat were really bad, the cotton would be coated with iodine! Obviously, very few sore throats were ever reported, and if they were, the cure was always immediate after one of these treatments.

Amalf

The word sounds so soothing, and, in truth, it was truly a wonderful home remedy. This was an all-purpose "medicine," which was "manufactured" on the kitchen stove by boiling certain leaves that grew wild in our backyard, until they produced a yellowish liquid. I was always more than willing to drink this substance as it tasted very good, especially when compared to the alternative drugstore-bought remedies such as castor oil (ugh), milk of magnesia (which truly tasted like chalk, and which even the promise of an Indian suit could not convince me to swallow), citrate of magnesia (which actually wasn't too bad), etc. I have often wondered what amalf actually was—it produced such a calming effect on you. Was it legal?

Backaches and Other Spinal Problems

We didn't have to go far for these cures . . . just downstairs to our maternal grandfather, Raphael, who had a special gift—he was the local chiropractor! He had no formal training, of course, but could expertly treat and cure (as far as I know) most ailments of the skeletal system, as long as you could pay him with a bottle of homemade wine. As with most Italian men, their "love of the grape" is legendary, as is their distaste for that awful-tasting substance—water. It must go back to the quality of water in their home country as they avoided it like the plague. My grandfather, as the story goes, stormed out of a doctor's office, on what was probably his first and last visit to a licensed physician, when the uninformed healer announced that he had "water-on-the-knee." He could envision no conceivable way in which that substance could have possibly entered his body to reside in his knee. I am sure he would have raised no objection should his condition been diagnosed as "wine-on-the-knee."

My Uncle Tuts, who, like most of my uncles, loved to play practical jokes, never tired of telling the story of my maternal grandmother's wake. He would have each mourner who went up to my grandfather to offer his or her condolences bring him a bottle of wine, which he tearfully placed behind his chair. You can imagine his reaction when he went to collect his stash at the end of the day to find that he only had one bottle. My uncle had secretly been recycling the same bottle as each person had come into the wake.

My grandfather had some unique chiropractic methods. He didn't have any actual equipment or even a table to put the "patients" on—but he did have his powerful back! I can remember coming home from school and seeing him in the middle of the kitchen with someone on his back and with their hands wrapped around his neck and their feet dangling a few feet from the floor. It must have worked—I know he didn't carry malpractice insurance!

The Neighborhood Pranks

Now that the Statute of Limitations has run out . . . hopefully . . . I can reveal for the first time some of the pranks unleashed on the inhabitants of the West, particularly by the infamous trio of me, Billy Williams, and Billy Rose.

Some of the more mundane activities included:

- Hotfoots—This involved creeping up behind someone and carefully putting the "action end" of a match into the small opening just above the soles of their shoes and lighting it. Dangerous? Of course . . . but was it fun to see them hopping up and down to put out the flame.
- Stink bombs—This required wrapping camera film (remember that) in a newspaper, lighting it, and throwing it into the center of a crowd. Dangerous? Of course . . . but was it fun to see everyone scramble to find some sweet-smelling, fresh air.
- Ringing doorbells—We usually did this in some of the apartment houses in the neighborhood, especially one at the corner of Union Avenue and Third Street, where I vividly remember gleefully ringing someone's bell very late at night and suddenly feeling a very strong grasp on my free arm. I turned to see the "intruder" . . . a one-armed man with the strongest grip I had ever felt . . . was I scared, as he kicked me in the ass and ended my bell-ringing nights . . . at least in that apartment.
- Letting the air out of tires—We would stick a matchstick (boy did we use these a lot) into the tire air valve of a car and sit in front of Mickey Moonlight's watching the air s . . . l . . . o . . . w . . . l . . . y . . . seep out of the tire, and then run like hell when the frustrated owner started looking around for the culprits.

Some of our more elaborate plots, however, required the planning and cunning of an escape from Alcatraz, such as our plan to seek revenge against our Third Street nemesis . . . Irish's (Contratta) mother. They lived just off to the right side of the goal line on our "football field," and it was not uncommon for a ball to wind up on their front lawn, generally after bouncing off the side of their home. Irish's mother didn't appreciate this and would keep our balls and threaten to call the cops, which she never actually did. In any event, we thought it was time to get some retribution for these adult intrusions into our "innocent" childhood pursuits, and thus devised an "innocent" childhood form of payback . . . a milk bottle filled with all sorts of human, and inhuman, waste, which we precipitously leaned against the front door to her home. Not only did we seek to escape detection when she answered the doorbell, but wanted to witness, and hear, her reaction as the contents of the bottle spilled onto her once-beautiful carpet—we were evil. As you have heard, Billy Williams was fast, but we now asked him to do the impossible—place the object at the doorstep, ring the bell, and dash up the street to our "observation lair" in front of Billy Rose's house on Washington Avenue. He did it . . . and after experiencing the loudest outcry we would ever hear from a human, we slithered off to a prearranged escape route which wound through several backyards, over and under several fences and walls, and left us right in front of Mickey Moonlight's, where everyone was discussing what had happened at Irish's mother's house . . . really?

All of our escapades, however, did not have successful endings, like the time we decided that the inhabitants of the "Old Men's Club" on Fourth Street needed a little excitement in their lives. We should have spent more time in planning our moves, but the anticipation of our "visit" was just too overwhelming to delay, and so we boldly walked to the front door of the club, opened it, and hurled eggs at the astonished senior citizens. I don't believe their arteries had pumped blood so freely in years, as the smashed eggs careened off walls, pictures, chairs, checkerboards, and various parts of their bodies. They might have been old (defined by us as anyone over twenty-five), but they could still use the phone, and before we had gone two blocks, a police car, with a flashing light and loud siren, pulled up to the curb, and a very agitated Officer Cappellino rushed up to us—oh boy! He was furious as he made outlandish accusations against us, which we of course vehemently denied, claiming we were just returning from a novena at the church. Anyway, what made him possibly think it was us? . . . to which he shouted, "Twenty eyewitnesses say they saw three boys throw the eggs: a small skinny kid with glasses, a tall skinnier kid with flaming-red hair and freckles, and the fattest kid they had ever seen"—talk about your circumstantial evidence. After confessing to our "mistake," in exchange for a promise not to tell our mothers, we agreed to go back to the club to clean up the mess, and to take a few shots in the back of the head from some of the more offended seniors. I truly believe, however, that this was one of the most exciting things to have happened to them in years!

The Habits

Most of the neighborhood kids had some type of habit, generally involving a facial tick or scratching some part of their body. My habit was clearly unique not only in the West, but in any other part of the known world. I have absolutely no clue as to how I developed it, and I will try my best to describe it—here it goes. At any time of the day or night (I was ok when I was sleeping) I would get an uncontrollable urge to stop whatever I was doing and touch the ground with the fingers of my two hands (again, I was chubby, but agile) and then "have to" touch my knees, chest, lips and forehead, in that precise order. This made it especially difficult when the "urge" came on me as I was running from the scene of the many pranks I have just described—besides, I always had a dirty face.

Other Characters

You have already heard about many of the characters in the neighborhood, but a few others merit special mention.

Bubba

Bubba (Trotta) was a large individual who had been blinded in an industrial accident (or so I believe). He was amazingly happy-go-lucky in spite of his affliction and took our endless, good-natured teasing without ever appearing to be upset by it—he was definitely a "character!" He lived on Third Street with his father who seemed to spend all his time sitting on the front porch. Bubba would always greet him with a short whistle and shouting out, "Hey, ghoul-a-se Pepe. You like-a him?" To which his father would always reply, "Wellllllll, I dono?"

He would occasionally fill in behind the counter at Mickey Moonlight's stationery store. I always believed he had some very slight vision and asked him about it one day, as I watched him make change for a pack of cigarettes. He laughingly explained that although he couldn't see, he could tell the difference in the coins by their size and in the bills by "feeling Lincoln's beard."

We would love to "tease" him by coming into the store and silently standing in front of him until he realized someone was there. On one occasion, an unsuspecting customer, not realizing Bubba's lack of sight, similarly stood there waiting for him to say something, which, of course, was not forthcoming. After a few moments, Bubba sensing that someone was there, and reasonably assuming it to be one of us, reached out and grabbed the poor soul in a bear-hug. It isn't too difficult to picture the surprise and unbridled fright experienced by this lost customer as he struggled free and went running out of the store, the neighborhood, the city, etc.

Although I did not actually see it happen, I was told that some of his "friends" drove him through the West in a convertible with what Bubba thought was a beautiful, blond woman on his lap—actually, it was a well-known black hooker!

He was, in the final analysis, one of the most interesting and caring characters in the West I was ever to meet, and I always had great admiration and respect for him. He was our true friend.

Louie "Chicken-Breast"

One of Bubba's constant companions was little Louie "Chicken Breast," who was his "eyes" and led him everywhere. It is difficult to actually describe what Louie looked like—he was dwarflike in size with a protruding chest and a rather large head full of black, shiny hair. Bubba, of course, never actually saw him and, on one occasion, playfully grabbed him (that again) by the head. He later asked us what Louie looked like as, in his words, "Jesus, it felt like he has a valley in the middle of his head."

Bubba, Louie, and a third partner whose name was also Louie decided to go into the Christmas tree business one winter. The only problem was that the new Louie was also blind—obviously, the venture was doomed to fail and, of course, did.

Stump-and-a-half

A reader may be assuming that we had a lot of laughs at the expense of some poor, handicapped individuals. This was certainly never our intent. They were just there and accepted as they were, except that they, like almost everyone else in the neighborhood, had a nickname, which was generally linked to their physical appearance, which, in each case, was obvious.

Stump-and-a-half, of course, only had one leg. He operated a stationery store at the intersection of Washington Avenue and Third Street, and when we weren't at Mickey Moonlight's, we were there. He, however, didn't stay in business very long, but for us street urchins, it was an unforgettable experience, as he not only taught us how to calculate the day's "number" from the attendance at various horse-racing tracks around the country, but, to his detriment, actually left us in charge of the store on occasions. He would return, and a glow would appear on his face when he saw how much of the candy stock we had apparently sold—the smile quickly dissolved, however, as soon as he opened the cash draw! He had great candy!

The "number" I just mentioned isn't the same as those boring tickets now sold legally all over the country. Everyone played the "numbers," and they were engrained in the daily life and dreams of us all. And I do mean dreams, especially if someone claimed to have had one of a specific number—everyone would play it. It wasn't necessary, however, to have such a precise dream, as they all could be converted into a number by reference to "dream books" available for sale at any stationery store.

The odds were great—six hundred to one (I believe) if you "hit" the three-digit number "straight" or half that if you hit any "combination" of the number. You could also play just the last number, referred to as "the drop." Typically, you would play for a nickel or a quarter, but if you really felt good about a number, you might risk a dollar. How did you play the numbers? You simply walked into the nearest stationery store and placed a bet by writing the number down on a small piece of paper, together with your wager. The store clerk then recorded your choices and the bets were collected by "runners." I actually never knew whom these runners reported to, but it must have been the "black hand." We never heard them referred to as the "Mafia," or the "Cosa Nostra"—the media created these names. I only knew one member of the "black hand", and he was eventually found in the front seat of a Cadillac . . . shot in the back of the head. The alleged owner of the car, whom I will not identify, as I value my life, has appeared in the pages of my story. As I have already mentioned, crime was rare in the West, although this same individual (who owned the aforementioned Cadillac) served time on the infamous "chain gang", and my parents would tell stories about a criminal, who lived in the apartment house where Billy Williams and his family lived, who went to the electric chair.

The numbers were, of course, illegal, and occasionally there would be a police raid on a selected store. These, however, were seldom successful as the whole neighborhood was vigilant for these attempts and someone would generally warn the store owner, who would usually flush the evidence down the toilet, or, if there were no alternative, eat the slips.

Another thing we liked about Stump-and-a-half's place was the back room where we could play our favorite card game—briscola. The game was best played in teams of two. Each player would put down a card, from the three which were dealt out, and it was up to the next player to try to beat it. All the cards did not have the same value, of course, and if you didn't have a "strong" hand, you would have your partner "leash," namely play a card with little or no value. If you had a good hand, however, especially a three, "the momma," or an ace, "the poppa," you would have him put down his highest point cards. The only problem was you were not allowed by the rules to let your partner know what you had in your hand, and the true artistry of the game was to devise a series of "signals" so that you could surreptitiously get him this information. A tug on the right ear could mean you had the "mamma," or a wink could signal the "poppa," and so on. You, of course, had to make sure the opposing team didn't intercept these signals, and therefore they had to be constantly changed. Autee (Cagliastro) was the reigning briscola champ, and he was almost invincible.

Someone, however, must have tipped off the cops that Stump-and-a-half was running card games in the back room, and a raid was made on the store one fateful day—what a mistake? The only two people in the back room at the time were Sonny Mecca, whom you already met, and another legend in his own time, Rocco (Zipilli). Sonny Mecca was hard to truly describe—Rocco is almost as impossible! About the only thing I might say is that he was insignificantly more understandable than Sonny Mecca. Try to picture the scene that greeted the police as they stormed into the back room—Sonny Mecca was playing solitaire in his inimitable fashion, while Rocco was quietly reading . . . the phone book. If you thought the Iron Horse could cry, as you will soon see, he was an amateur next to the antics of this tandem as the police unwisely attempted to "bring them downtown." These characters defied understanding when they were in complete command of their faculties, so imagine what came out of their mouths between mournful sobs and wailings. That was the last raid ever attempted at Stump-and-a-half's!

The Iron Horse

One of the runners was the Iron Horse (Joseph Storino) who "earned" that name from his early days in the boxing ring when he would fight several times in one night. At a reunion organized by Marie (Skippers) Pirro held in New Rochelle in November 2002, I was to learn from Mike Cakouros, the husband of Mickey Moonlight's daughter, Rose, that the Iron Horse was in "Ripley's Believe It or Not," as the only person ever to fight in four matches in two nights in two states. We never saw him in his prime, but he was a large hulk of a man who walked with a slow shuffle and could only look to the side by turning his whole body around—legend had it that a cement bag fell on his neck and left him in that state—actually I believe it was from an automobile accident.

Another distinguishing feature was the way in which he spoke—he always sounded as though he was crying (maybe he always was?) We were told he did get "picked up" on one occasion for running the numbers and was brought down to the police station to appear before a judge. After hearing the Iron Horse cry for several minutes, the judge screamed at the arresting officer to not only let him go, but to never bring him before the court again, no matter what he did.

All of Them

There was an endless array of other characters that inhabited the West and an inexhaustible number of stories identified with them, but I leave them for someone else to tell. My last legacy to the descendants of the West is to list the nicknames of those that I, and others, could think of. I know we didn't get them all.

NICKNAMES OF CHARACTERS INCLUDED IN THE BOOK (*FAMILY)

Ascadole
Autee (Cagliastro)
Babe (Branca)
*Baron and Tuts (Thomas Semenza)
Big Head (Denicola)
Bird Brain (Petrone)
Bobeep (Cassone)
Bubba (Trotta)
*Bumbo (Columbus DeRosa)
Charlie "the Jew" (Lerner)
*Chickencorn (Joe Calo)
Cooney (Silo)
Cookie (Noberto)
Chi Chi (DeLeo)
Dannyboy (Grosso)
Dave "the Jew"
Dee Dee (Tedesco)
*Dipip (Johnny DiPippo)
Porky (Grosso)
Dodo
Flea (Gentile)
*Fatass and Ponzie (Ralph DeRosa)
*Fuzzy (Alphonse Poggiale)
*Gabby (Ronnie Semenza)

*Gennerine (Gennero Poggiale)
Hank Deck (Declemente)
Irish (Contratta)
Iron Horse (Storino)
Ishkabibble (Mamone)
Joe Biff (Bevalaqua)
Joe Pisch (Piedmont)
Joe Rote (Rotyliano)
Johnny DeMaz (DeMasi)
*Junior and Joe College (Charlie Semenza)
Junior (Noberto)
Kenny Lib (Libertino)
Kentucky (Carino)
Leo "the Chicken Market" (Luiso)
*Looch (Carmela Calo)
Louie "Chicken Breast"
Louie "the Cake Shoppe" (Celestino)
Little Anna (Libertino)
*Ma (Mary Poggiale)
Matty (Amorasano)
Mickey Moonlight (Facazio)
Mico (Colangelie)
Mingo (Grosso)
*Murph (Vito Codella)
Musta Geed
Mutt and Jeff (Save-My-Soul)
*Noisey (Louis Semenza)
Nooch (D'Ermes)
Pissbones (Rispoli)
Pope (Grosso)
Professor (Cavalli)
Red (Hollis)
Sally (Colangelo)
Sammy Fish (Daniele)
Sam "the Watchman" (Mistruzzi)
Sonny Mecca
Seeley (Burigio)
Skinhead (Contratta)
Snake (Santacroce)

Stump-and-a-half
*Trattie (Gertrude Semenza)
*Vec (Donald Vecchio)

THE OTHERS

Acceleek
Ace
Adamando
Allyboy
Angelo Wheat

Banannas
Baseball and Nothing Else
Bangy
Batman
Benny Ack
Big Jim
Bill Hart
Bill T
Bing
Bishy
Bochain
Bokeek
Black Pete
Blade
Blimp
B O Platte
Bones
Brang 'Em
Brains
Brother
Buddy
Buffalo Head
Bull
Bullfrog
Bunky
Buster
Butch

Ca Ca
California
Canute
Cappy
Cazaaz
Cha Cha
Chapell
Charlie "My Boy"
Charmaine
Cheech
Cheeta
Cherry Head
Chet
Chicago
Chicago Bears
Chick-a-Rum
Chicken Head
Chickadee
Chief
Chink
Chip
Chip a Nay
Coozie
Coochie
Corky
Crack
Crabeulla
Crazy Mary
Crumby

Dee
Dell "the Tailor"
Dejock
Ditty
Dizzy
Do What
Doc
Donnie Zack

Donkey
Duchie
Duck Feet
Dutch

Eddie Cantor
Eddie Wool
Eggie (a.k.a. the Egg)

Farmer
Fat Frankie
Fats
Felix
Fez
Fig
Fifty-cents
Fleahole
Foe
Footsie
Four Eyes
Fox
Fordham
Frankie Eel
Freddie Rube
Funzy Leaps

Gate
Geets
Ginky
Glishy
Gooney
Goondale
Goo Goo
Goose
Grandma
Granny
Green Leaf
Green Shit

Hank T
Harry "Toothless Eye"
Hawk Eye
Hip
Honeyboy
Hooker
Husky
Hubble

Japan
Jazz
Jimmy A
Jimmy Dimps
Joe Beans
Joe Butch
Joe Butt
Joe Chan
Joe Crooked
Joe Runt
Joe Slick
Joe T
Joe the Baker
Joe V
Joey Orange
Johnny Big Wang
Johnny Boot
Johnny Church
Johnny Rex
Johnny Surge
J R
Jungle Jim

Kippy
Kissey

La La
Lizzie
Loeb
Lulu

Mafe
Mag
Mike "ala Bicycala"
Maneek
Marco ("Big" and "Little")
Mary Leeps
Mary Red
Matt "the Bat"
Maymay
Mcgee
Minny
Mickey "Shitey Eye"
Mikey Lib
Molly Brown
Monk
Mooch
Moo Cow
Moo Moo
Mosky
Mudrock
Mummy
Mundo
Mush

Nab
Narrow
Natty
Nello
Netta
Nickey Dieg
Nickey Sug
Ninny Brown
Nuncie

Olive Oil

Papa Joe
Peanuts

Pencil
Penooch
Piccolo
Pigeon
Piggy
Pinkey
Pipp
Pop
Popeye
Putalink
Puggy
Puttin Head

Radio Joe
Rail Hopper
Ramone
Red
Red the Peddler
Robert Taylor
Rocky

Sabitine
Sallyboy
Sam "the Peddler"
Santiago
Scacheet
Scoop
Scratch
Shadow
Six-O-Clock
Skippy
Sonny
Sonnyboy
Spud
Spita Eye
Stretch
Subir
Sundre
Syracuse

Tabac
Tarzan
Tex
Thaw Thaw
The Dancer
The Plunger
The Stroller
Tom Bear
Tomtom
Tootie
Tootsie
Tuffy
Tut

Untay

Wang Wang
Whitey
Wiggles
Willy Wink
Wood

Yammy
Yum Yum

Zeek
Ziarocca
Zit

and the "colored guys" who generally didn't have actual nicknames but were always referred to by their first and last names like Charlie Razor, Eddie Carolina, Chauncey Williams, Adolph Robinson, Ducky Robinson, Albert Seal, Jessie Brown, and Jackie Wells.

And, finally, me, Chesty!

The last photo is one of my favorites; it was taken in our backyard with my father and, heaven knows why, Aunt Gertie hanging out of the window (from whence Ronnie once fell)—now you can see why I was called Chesty!

BVG